What Goe

Also by Leann Richards and published by Ginninderra Press
Houdini's Tour of Australia
The First Merry Widow

Leann Richards

What Goes Up

Australian Juggling to World War I

For Jos, Kenny and Shiho

What Goes Up: Australian Juggling to World War I
ISBN 978 1 76109 317 3
Copyright © text Leann Richards 2022

First published 2022 by
GINNINDERRA PRESS
PO Box 3461 Port Adelaide 5015
www.ginninderrapress.com.au

Contents

Introduction

What is juggling? For the purposes of this history, juggling is broadly defined as the manipulation of objects. So this book discusses hoop rolling, plate spinning, traditional club and ball juggling, hat juggling and lots of balancing. There are also many discussions of individual jugglers, including international visitors like Cinquevalli and American minstrels like Joseph Jalvan. Australia also produced some incredible jugglers, including amazing circus performers like Marizles Wirth, international superstars like Stan Kavanagh, and local talents like Arnold Jarvis.

My aim with this book is to promote discussion about Australian juggling history in the hope that others will extend, refine and uncover more details. I have also purposefully concentrated on lesser known performers. So, for example, although the Ashton family greatly influenced Australian juggling, I have not discussed their role at length, primarily because so much has already been written about them. I have also limited the book to those whose career started before the Great War, primarily because it would take a decade, at least, to include juggling to the present day.

Finally, this book would not have been possible without the help of some wonderful historians: Dr Mark St Leon, without whom there would be no circus history in Australia; David Cain of the United States, who is the world's foremost juggling historian; and Erik Aberg, who is the absolute expert on Cinquevalli. All were astonishingly generous with their time and I am grateful for their patience, advice and help. I would also like to thank the family of Arnold (Arnoldi) Jarvis, particularly Trevor Hoath and Brenton Maile, who kindly made time to discuss their famous ancestor.

According to Kenny Cheung, Australian world record holding juggler, 'Juggling is not only an artform, but a skill or a sport. To me, juggling is everything.' All the jugglers mentioned here had one thing in common, a shared joy and passion for juggling. That passion inspires the few Australian jugglers who continue to juggle today. For us, juggling really is everything.

Before the British

Human beings have been manipulating objects for a very long time. The first visual evidence of a kind of juggling seems to be a set of pictograms found on a wall in the Beni Hassan tombs in Egypt. There are also tales of ancient Chinese warriors juggling swords in front of armies to prevent wars, stories of jugglers entertaining kings, queens and emperors, and accounts of impoverished people using juggling to extract coins from enraptured crowds.

There is also a history of juggling in the Pacific Islands. Women in Tonga have juggled for centuries. Their tradition originated with the story of a goddess of the underworld who would snatch, and juggle, the eyes of those who trespassed in her domain. The Tongans call this juggling Hiko, and it is practised primarily by women.

Long before the English came to Australia in 1788, there were thriving communities of Indigenous people on the continent and, like many communities, their culture included play. Unfortunately, much of that Indigenous culture was destroyed after 1788 and most accounts of Indigenous play were written by the colonisers. Those accounts include stories about Indigenous games, which suggest that the Aboriginal people of Australia played with and manipulated many different objects. Among the games were skipping, string games, ball games, top spinning, and fire games. It is easy to extrapolate some sort of juggling from this list.

Therefore, although not a proven fact, it seems reasonable to suggest that the first jugglers on the Australian continent were Indigenous people. Given that they have been in Australia for over forty thousand years, juggling could possibly be one of the oldest activities ever pursued by humankind.

The Convict Jugglers

The idea of juggling as it is known today is a relatively new one. Before the mid-nineteenth century, juggling was used as a synonym for deception or trickery. Jugglery was frowned upon as the art of the criminal.

In 1788, a fleet of ships carrying convicts from England arrived in Gadigal country, which the English later called Sydney. Thus began the European invasion of Australia. It is possible that some of those convicts and perhaps some of the crew manipulated objects for entertainment. It is even more probable that some of the passengers were involved in jugglery in the more nefarious sense.

Among the convicts were several musicians, singers and actors. In the early years of the colony, there were scattered accounts of ad hoc performances in ale houses, inns and in some private homes. However, theatrical activity in a formal capacity was frowned upon as a morally corrupting influence, and although there was some early convict theatre, an officially authorised industry was not permitted until around the 1830s.

One of the earliest convict colonies was the penal settlement of Van Diemen's Land (Tasmania), and its most feared gaol was Port Arthur, a harsh prison which employed convicts as slave labour. The worst criminals were sent there, the irredeemable, the recidivists, those doomed to a lifetime of servitude.

Next to these ruffians and hoodlums lived a small coterie of officers' wives and families who needed to be kept occupied while their husbands kept order. Among these were William Champ, commandant, and Thomas Lempriere, his assistant. Lempriere had several children, and in mid-1848 he obtained a pass for a convict to visit his house to entertain the family. The convict entertainer was Joseph Crapp.

Joseph, also known as Joseph Pain, was a short, dark-complected ex-sailor with tattoos of women and anchors etched on his arms, and inked bracelets around his wrists. Joseph stole a hat in Devon, England, was caught, and in 1831, at the age of twenty-two, was transported to Australia for fourteen years.

Upon arrival in the colony, Joseph was assigned a job. Shortly afterwards, he entered the 'dwelling house of Mrs M Reid taking improper liberties with her person when she was in bed' and was sentenced to twelve months' hard labour for the crime. Subsequently, he was assigned as a shepherd, but he deserted the sheep; when he was a watchman, he deserted the post. He was convicted of laziness, absconding, drunkenness and stealing an accordion. He was not a model citizen.

However, he was a performer, and in 1848, he visited Thomas Lempriere to perform juggling tricks. What he performed or how well he performed is not recorded.

Ten years later, he was arrested for juggling.

In 1858, Joseph was a ticket of leave man. He was on probation and could be employed. He was working at the Lukerman Inn in Hobart and one night the landlord opened his doors for a grand ball. During the evening, Joseph started exhibiting juggling tricks in the ballroom. This was illegal, and Joseph was charged with 'misconduct, as a prisoner of the crown, in juggling in a public room'. He was given a warning and told not to juggle in public. He was, perhaps, the first person to be arrested for juggling in Australia.

In January 1861, Joseph was charged with juggling again. This time in Launceston. Joe and his mate George Smith arrived in town without telling the authorities, as they were required to do as ex-felons. Instead, they toured the local tap rooms and pubs as jugglers and conjurors. After visiting several establishments and asking for compensation for their performances, the two men slowly made their way to the police station to sign in. They were promptly arrested for misconduct. This time, Joseph was convicted and sentenced to a month's hard labour.

Unfortunately, Joe's days as a juggler were numbered. In April 1861, a large tub of butter crashed on his head and killed him. The incident was deemed an accident and it ended the career of Joseph Crapp, juggler.

It is unlikely that Joe was the only convict juggler. Another convict, John Harrop in Sydney, was described as a calico printer and juggler when he absconded from custody in the 1840s. John was apprehended in a pub, where he was, perhaps, plying the juggling trade. It seems, therefore, that entertainment in the inns and pubs of the early colony involved juggling among other amusements.

Another famous juggling convict was Golding Ashton, the founder of the famous Ashton Circus. Golding, aka James Ashton, was one of the earliest circus proprietors and, as a juggler, introduced the fine art into the circus in Australia.

The Early Circus Jugglers

Australian circus can trace its origins to Radford's Royal Circus in Launceston in 1847. The circus had equestrians, acrobats, tumblers and rope-walkers. By the 1850s and the gold rush, there were several circuses touring the land, and many of them included jugglers.

One of the early exponents of circus in Australia was James Henry Ashton. Ashton and his descendants trained many local jugglers who later performed on Australian stages. James was a circus proprietor and included jugglers in his shows from the very beginning. As early as 1849, in Melbourne, he held a benefit which featured Monsieur Risley, a juggler. By 1852, Ashton was in New South Wales and promising juggling, balancing and acrobatic feats for audiences.

Ashton seems to have performed Risley juggling – that is, juggling people with the feet. This type of juggling was named after Richard Risley Carlisle, who introduced it in the USA in the early 1840s. This was not the same Risley featured in Ashton's show, although Ashton did not say this in his advertising. In addition to juggling people, Ashton also juggled objects with his feet, and this is known as foot juggling. Ashton popularised foot juggling in early Australia and one of his apprentices, Robert Taylor, was well known for his skill in the art.

Taylor, born in Windsor, New South Wales, was foot juggling in Sydney in 1855, firstly with Ashton and then with Burton's circus. In 1857, Taylor performed at the goldfields in Bendigo, Victoria, with Burton. In this show, he put a large ball 'through a variety of evolutions moving it with the same facility with his feet as if they were his hands'. He also stilt-walked and balanced on a large globe while juggling.

Ashton was not the only circus proprietor at the time. In Sydney, there was another circus, Malcolm's Royal Australian Amphitheatre. At

Malcolm's, they had a house juggler called Signor Cardoza, the juggling king, who performed a 'grand juggling act on a courser', a horse.

Another competitor who arrived around 1852 was Henry Burton. On Boxing Day that year,he provided performers for a grand fete at the Sir Joseph Banks Hotel at Botany Bay, in Sydney. It featured his great equestrian artistes, including Major John Downey, who juggled while his horse galloped at full speed, and an equilibrist (balancer) who, on the back of a white horse, spun plates and manipulated other items.

It seems that object manipulation was a major part of the circus tradition, although only a tangential part of the show. Juggling complemented feats of equestrian acrobatics and most circus performers probably included it in their skill set.

The discovery of gold in Australia changed everything for entertainers in the country. It brought wealth, thousands of people, and a multicultural mix to the small insular society. This resulted in a higher demand for shows, and many circuses responded by becoming itinerant and visiting the goldfields, chasing the money of those chasing their dream.

With the desire for more entertainment came the need for more performers. One way the circus met the demand was by adopting or acquiring unwanted Aboriginal or part-Aboriginal children. One of these children was a young boy nicknamed 'Little Nugget'. In 1852, the youngster was juggling with Burton's circus near the goldfields at the Commercial Hotel, Bathurst. He performed as one of the Jugglers of Antwerp, 'spinning plates and throwing balls'.

'Little Nugget' was the seven-year-old child of an Anglo man called William and an Indigenous woman known only as Mary Ann. As the son of a white and Indigenous person, he was very low on the social scale. He was one of many children who were illegally 'adopted' by the circus, as there was little regulation over child welfare at the time.

Soon he was renamed Billy Jones, after John Jones, a former Burton employee who left to form his own circus and took the child with him. Billy performed in several circuses under various names and was the first documented Aboriginal person to perform in a circus. He was an acrobat, juggler, equestrian, rope-walker and superb performer.

By the 1860s, circus had become a featured entertainment in Australia and juggling was a part of the show. These early jugglers were some of the first to introduce the skill to large audiences.

It took some time for juggling to find its way from the circus and itinerant performers to the stage, and it was not until the 1860s that juggling found a home there. Not surprisingly, juggling, an art form that was associated with outsiders, became associated with the mysterious East and was a part of the nineteenth-century fascination with all things Japanese.

The Japanese Jugglers

The English empire in the Victorian era included the grand prize of India. Perceptions of India and other Asian nations at that time revolved around a conviction of Anglo superiority and Eastern exoticism and difference. The opening of Japan to the west in the 1860s led to a craze for Japanese culture that was heavily influenced by these attitudes.

Juggling as skill or art form had long been associated with Indian exoticism. Early Australian newspapers contain many accounts of Indian jugglers, who were snake charmers and acrobats. The association of juggling with the otherness and mystery of the east, reinforced the idea of juggling as an outsider art.

Australian theatre proliferated during the 1850s and 1860s and this coincided with the opening of Japan to the Western world. It is not surprising, therefore, that the stage was used to expose Japanese culture to the colony.

Capitalising on the Western interest in all things Eastern, enterprising entrepreneurs began to organise Japanese touring groups to Australia. Most of these included jugglers, plate spinners and balancers. In 1867, two Japanese touring groups arrived in Australia.

The first was the Tycoon group, which consisted of five men and two women and exhibited top spinning, balancing and juggling. They wore traditional Japanese clothing and were introduced by an interpreter, who spoke in broken English. This troupe specialised in top spinning. They threw tops over five and a half metres and caught them on the palm of the hand, balanced them on the edge of a sword and spun three along a long cord. They also manipulated boxes and performed butterfly fanning. This group appeared in Sydney, Adelaide and Melbourne, and in provincial centres of Victoria.

At the same time, a second troupe, the Dragon Troupe, toured Australia. This group was imported by entrepreneurs Thomas Lenton and his partner Smith, who recruited the performers in Yokohama. They had some difficulty getting permission to include the female artists but after some high-level pressure, the women could leave Japan. The troupe consisted of around eleven people, with women, children and two jugglers, including one called Gengero or Genjiro. It was a family affair, with a baby born during the sea voyage to Australia and Gengero's wife having a child, their second, during the tour.

Gengero was a balancer and a juggler. He balanced a long bamboo stick on his shoulder, as one of the children climbed to the top and performed acrobatic feats. He also did some traditional juggling, tossing balls and knives and catching them 'with surprising adroitness'. He was a talented top spinner and amazed audiences with his ability to balance a spinning top on the edge of a bamboo stick.

The other juggler, Bungero, a pedal equilibrist, or foot juggler, juggled a screen with his feet as one of the children wandered around the outside of it. He also balanced a tub while on his back as a child acrobat performed contortions on it.

The troupe performed in full traditional clothing and included the butterfly trick in their act. This involved making a paper butterfly swoop around the stage and perch upon a woman's hand. The number of butterflies grew as the act progressed and eventually the stage was filled with colourful butterflies fluttering around the amphitheatre. They later added a kabuki show. The sound of Japanese music contributed to the atmosphere, one critic calling it 'a constant scrape on a pair of fiddles'.

They played to packed houses in Melbourne, Adelaide and Sydney, including an appearance at the prestigious Princess Theatre in Melbourne. Japan had only allowed its people to travel recently, so these early troupes were pioneers who brought their unique brand of juggling to Western audiences. Their success led to the arrival of other groups with similar programmes.

In 1871, the Satsuma group from Osaka came to Australia. Their featured juggler was Matz Noski, a pedal equilibrist who balanced six tubs on his feet. However, the undoubted star of the show was 'All Right', a warm and funny young boy, who stood atop the tubs, doing acrobatics. 'All Right' was mentioned approvingly in all reviews of the show.

In 1873, another Japanese troupe, known by various names, including the Royal Tycoon group, came to Australia. The juggler of this group, Decenoski, also known as Sakagawa Rikinosuike, is widely acknowledged as the first recorded Japanese naturalised citizen of Australia. Although described as an 'acrobat' by many researchers, he was recorded as a 'juggler' on his entrance visa. He requested naturalisation from the Queensland colonial government in 1882.

In the show, Decenoski balanced a ladder or bamboo pole while one of the children, Ewar, climbed it and performed acrobatics on top. The trick involved Decenoski placing the ladder on his shoulder. Ewar climbed the rungs, one by one, and after reaching the top, he twirled and twisted and jumped, contorting his body into different shapes. Suddenly, half the ladder fell away, leaving Deconoski balancing a single pole. Ewar continued his acrobatics as he was precariously perched on this slim stick. This was the first performance of the act in Australia.

Decenoski married an Australian woman and remained in the country, performing in circuses. Eventually, he formed his own troupe with his wife and children. His petition for naturalisation came two years before his death in 1884.

The child who climbed the ladder, Ewar, also remained in Australia, married a local woman, and formed his own circus under the name of his mentor and friend, Decenoski (now spelt Dicinoski).

Ewar's troupe was involved in a spy scandal in 1908 which illustrated the suspicions the Australian people had for those who were different in race and occupation. The same scandal captured another famous Japanese juggler in its talons.

In 1908, the famous Maskelyne and Devant company of England

sent a touring troupe to Australia and New Zealand. One member of the group was the famous Japanese juggler, Gintaro.

Gintaro Nizuhara, or Gintaro Mitzuhara, was a Japanese man who had lived in England for twenty-one years. He was married to an English woman, Isabella, and originally worked as a merchant. Around 1900, he started working for the Maskelyne and Devant Mysteries show. He spun a silver ring around an umbrella, spun and balanced tops and perched a tub on top of a pole. The highlight of his act was balancing a glass on top of twenty-eight bricks and catching the glass as the bricks tumbled to the floor. He performed dressed in full Japanese traditional costume, adding to the mystery element of the show.

After a successful tour of Australia, the company, with Gintaro, travelled to New Zealand in early 1909. While they were there, a scandal erupted in Australia revolving around some travelling Japanese show people.

The Australian defence minister was travelling in Queensland when he was accosted by some stockmen and told a tale about a group of suspicious Japanese itinerant performers who were entertaining at the properties in the area. The men toured with a cinematograph, took pictures, and asked questions about the location of stations, waterholes, tracks and other landmarks. The showmen were accused by squatters, the stockmen, the newspapers and the minister of being spies in the pay of the Japanese government.

After this incident, for two years, every Japanese person who toured that part of the country had to be reported by the police to the government. Records show that the Dicinoski group were caught in the net and their movements were monitored and dutifully reported by the local police.

This fear of the Japanese caused Gintaro some trouble in New Zealand.

Gintaro kept a diary of his tours which he supplemented with photos of all the places he played. When Maskelyne and Devant arrived in Gisborne, a port in New Zealand, he took pictures of the port and the ships in the harbour. To his surprise, the innocent photography trip led to a letter being published in the local paper. The author, anonymous of course, accused Gintaro of spying. The newspaper breathlessly reported that half an hour after the arrival of a warship, Gintaro was spotted 'perched on the small crane on the breakwater, taking photographs, up and down and across the river'.

Gintaro gave an interview to defend his actions. 'I think it is a most childish thing to say,' he told the paper and added that pictures of the port and town were easily available at the local shops. Gintaro asserted that his business was that of a juggler and if he was a spy, he would not be using a camera where everybody could see it.

The newspaper asked him about an 'Asiatic invasion' and he replied that Japan was England's friend and would certainly aid New Zealand if any invasion occurred.

He concluded the interview with a broad smile, saying,

Twenty pound a week for entertaining was far ahead of what the Japanese Government would give any person for travelling around taking photographs…and that they [English-speaking people] could rest assured that he would do or say nothing that would offer them the slightest insult.

Gintaro completed his tour of New Zealand without any further accusations of spying, but the incident was an example of attitudes which he must have encountered frequently throughout his long and successful juggling career.

Japanese jugglers and the Japanese tradition played a large role in juggling in the Australian colonies. They represented part of the Japanese cultural craze which swept the Western world in the mid-nineteenth century. They also brought skills such as balancing, top spinning and variations of foot juggling to Australian audiences and juggling practitioners. Notably they performed in major theatres in Australia, bringing aspects of the juggling art into the more formal atmosphere of the stage. These performers were true pioneers and their influence was strong throughout the golden age of juggling in the early twentieth century.

There was another group who also influenced the development of the Australian juggling tradition. They too were regarded as exotic outsiders who performed miraculous feats and were subject to the racist stereotypes of the times. These were the minstrels, who were immensely popular with Australian audiences.

The Minstrel Performers

The first minstrel performers played in Australia in 1849 and they were a popular feature of colonial entertainment during the gold rush era. Both American and English based troupes toured the country, but it was not until the 1890s that a distinctly variety flavour became attached to the genre. With this turn towards variety, came the minstrel jugglers, including Joseph Jalvan and John Pamplin.

Even after the American Civil War, African-American performers were restricted from appearing on American stages with white entertainers. Thus, troupes of minstrels made up entirely of Black Americans formed and they became vehicles for musicians, singers and dancers to become professionally famous and prosperous.

Unlike the United States, there was no segregation in Australian theatres. Black performers could share the stage with their white peers with no restrictions except local prejudice. Many former minstrels, such as Irving Sayles, remained in Australia after their troupes left the country because they felt they had more opportunities. Sayles soon became a well-loved, popular and wealthy figure on the Australian Tivoli Circuit.

Joseph Jalvan and John Pamplin were two jugglers who worked together with McCabe's Minstrels in Philadelphia in 1890 and in Cuba in 1891–92. In the latter country, Jalvan was so popular that an admirer presented him with a diamond pin.

In 1897, the remarkable Orpheus McAdoo, a former child slave turned theatrical entrepreneur, was looking for additions for his show which was touring South Africa. One of the people he recruited for that trip was the popular juggler, Joseph Jalvan.

According to his wedding certificate, Jalvan was born Joseph O'Bryan in 1862. He worked as an 'Egyptian Juggler' with McCabe in the early 1890s, after which he joined McAdoo and travelled to South Africa. While there, he performed a juggling feat with a lighted lamp that was described as a 'marvel of dexterity'. He was tremendously successful, but the rumblings of the Boer War forced McAdoo and his party to travel to Australia.

McAdoo's Jubilee Singers arrived in 1898. They came prepared to emphasise the 'exotic' nature of the group, choosing to present their show with a 'Moorish' theme. Jalvan juggled plates and balls, and spun tops, but it was his balancing which caused the most applause. He put one pipe in his mouth, placed another pipe on top of it, placed a bottle on top of that and a lighted lamp on a stick-on top of the bottle. Then, after carefully steadying the whole contraption with his hand, he removed it and balanced the lot precariously just holding the bottom pipe in his mouth. In Newcastle, near Sydney, the newspapers said that Jalvan's act was alone worth the price of admission.

In late 1899, Jalvan with several of his fellow performers parted ways with McAdoo and formed their own minstrel company. They toured the provincial areas of Australia and were quite successful. He was also successful in love. He married a local woman, Catherine Webb, the same year.

The next year, he signed a contract with the most popular variety circuit in the country, the Tivoli Circuit. He was now performing for a world-class theatre company which hosted major international stars. He was no longer the exotic 'Moor', he was now the 'eastern' or 'Oriental wonderworker'. In Sydney, he wore a Japanese costume and balanced various objects, including a live pigeon on a trellis of clay pipes, with the bottom pipe held between his teeth.

His work was praised as 'skilful and spirited' and his stage persona was 'bright and appealing'. At the Tivoli, he was well paid, played to packed houses and received warm applause every night.

Eventually, Mr and Mrs Jalvan left Australia. He continued to juggle and balance in the United States and was working up to 1929.

Jalvan's departure from McAdoo left the entrepreneur with a juggling spot to fill, and he returned to the United States to find a replacement. On that trip, in St Louis, he found another juggler, John Pamplin.

Pamplin was a popular and experienced juggler who had toured Cuba with McCabe's Minstrels when Jalvan was part of the show. After that, he worked with the Georgia Graduates Company, which was a variety group active between 1895 and 1897. In the former year, they toured the north of the United States and followed this with a transcontinental run in 1897. One of the lead performers on that tour was Ernest Hogan, one of the early proponents of ragtime.

Pamplin arrived in Australia as part of a group including singer Flora Batson and contortionist (William) Ferry the Frog. He joined McAdoo's new troupe, grandly titled 'The Georgia Minstrels and Alabama Cakewalkers'.

In Australia, Pamplin maintained the tradition of 'exotic' juggler by wearing 'ancient Egyptian dress', which was 'distinctively novel'. He performed sleight of hand and 'equipoise', which was 'skilled', 'unique' and 'clever'. He also replicated Jalvan's act and carried a pet pigeon and a cannonball.

However, his most famous feat was gun juggling and manipulation. He dressed in a Zouave uniform and juggled firstly one, then two guns, making them 'fly all around and over him in the most bewildering style'. In Australia, Pamplin was regarded as being as highly skilled as Cinquevalli and was repeatedly praised by the press for his unusual and rare tricks. He was clearly a very accomplished and skilled juggler.

He was also a club juggler. In South Australia in 1899, he gave an exhibition of club swinging. That same year, during a performance at the Theatre Royal in Adelaide, he included club swinging and juggling in the show. This is one of the earliest records of club juggling in an Australian theatre.

Pamplin left Australia after the tour and continued working in the United States. In 1912, his juggling persona was 'his satanic majesty, the devil'. In 1929, he performed with a Wild West show, and his finale was balancing a revolving table on a pole attached to his chin. In the same show, he apparently juggled clubs, balls and blocks.

He died on 27 February 1935 in Danville, Illinois.

The minstrel jugglers continued the tradition of associating juggling with exotic and mysterious eastern locales. They dressed in extravagant costumes and thrilled Australian audiences with their unusual balancing and twirling feats. Their later performances occurred at the same time as juggling was about to become one of the most popular acts on the Australian stage. Just as Pamplin and Jalvan were leaving, another man, a European, was about to introduce the Australian public to a unique and marvellous juggling act.

The Vaudeville Jugglers

Juggling rose to prominence in the theatre during the early twentieth century with the emergence of variety and vaudeville circuits around the world. The most popular juggling act during that time was what is today called the 'gentleman juggler', a man who juggled everyday objects in unusual ways. The man who brought this style of juggling to Australia and heralded a wave of international practitioners and local imitators was Cinquevalli, who was one of the most popular performers to ever grace an Australian theatre.

Cinquevalli, however, would not have come to Australia without the support of another man, former music hall performer Harry Rickards. The arrival of English-born Harry Rickards in Australia in 1892 led to the rise of one of the most famous and lucrative variety theatre circuits in the world, the Australian Tivoli Circuit. Rickards imported some of the best variety acts to the young nation and ensured that the country experienced the popular theatre boom that conquered the west in the early twentieth century. It was through Rickards that Australian audiences saw world-class performers such as Houdini, Chung Ling Soo, and jugglers such as Cinquevalli, W.C. Fields, Salerno and Kara.

Cinquevalli

Cinquevalli was the most famous, but perhaps not the most skilful, juggler in the world during the early twentieth century, and he was one of the best at self-promotion. In Australia, he was considered the foremost exponent of the art of juggling of household items. It is through Cinquevalli that juggling was accepted on the vaudeville stage in Australia. He spread the skill through the country, he inspired many to follow him, and he was long remembered in theatrical circles for his good humour,

1. Paul Cinquevalli

generosity and intelligence. Cinquevalli's respectable demeanour off stage made juggling more acceptable to white middle-class audiences, who demanded that he return again and again to entertain and delight them. The impact of Cinquevalli on juggling in Australia cannot be overstated.

He visited the country four times between 1899 and 1914 and was a huge success on each occasion.

'I like Australia,' he said during his 1909 visit. 'Who could not like a country like this – not only the place and the climate – but look at the audiences and how do they treat me.'

Cinquevalli was an expert at self-promotion and his biography should be assessed in this light. Like many a performer, he exaggerated and embellished his life story for publicity purposes. What is true and what is fantasy is hard to determine with Cinquevalli.

Most agree that he was born in Poland around 1859, but his birth name is disputed. However, he eventually became Paul Cinquevalli and that is what he liked to be called.

What is not disputed is the accident that transformed him from trapeze artist to juggler. He called it 'the fluke of my life'.

When performing in St Petersburg on the flying trapeze, one of the assistants forgot to wipe the bar of one of the trapezes, and when I swung across space and gripped, my hands slipped. I knew how to fall, that was part of our training then, but in the downward course I struck one of the wires supporting the poles and this upset my balance and I fell in a heap.

Juggling was always part of Cinquevalli's repertoire, and he often juggled and performed sleight of hand in private. After the accident, his friends urged him to take it up as a profession. He began to juggle ordinary items like matches, cigars and umbrellas and worked his way up to specialty items. He soon became one of the foremost jugglers of his generation

He was a charming conversationalist with a down-to-earth manner. *Theatre Magazine* in Sydney called him 'unassuming and brilliant'. He was 'above average height and well proportioned'. As was expected of a former aerialist, he was graceful and fluid in his movements and had a charismatic stage presence. He had a variety of skills. He was a weight-lifter, an expert mandolinist and an accomplished linguist, and had a phenomenal memory. His ability to memorise long columns of figures was often remarked upon.

The juggler was also a skilled raconteur. In 1909, he told a story about escaping a murderous lunatic who had tried to throw him from an enormous building. It was a 'thrilling and blood curdling' tale according to his listeners. He had a self-deprecating sense of humour which was demonstrated in the articles he wrote for local magazines. His control of his image was masterful.

But he was more than just stories and publicity. He was one of the most unique and gifted jugglers of the age. He invented many of his routines and put an unusual spin on those he stole. He juggled with billiard balls while holding in his teeth, a table, a chair and Walter Burford, his assistant. One year, he had a pony cart driven on stage and then balanced it on his chin. In another trick, he balanced a top hat on an umbrella and perched on top of the hat was a half-crown coin and a cigar. He tossed the whole bundle in the air and caught the cigar in his mouth, the coin in his right eye and the hat on his head.

Cinquevalli had two famous feats and performed both in Australia. The first was the cannonball trick in which he caught a twenty-two-kilogram cannonball, suspended about two metres above his head, on his neck. (The actual weight of the cannonball has been disputed.) He got the idea by accident when practising one day.

> When I was balancing a large wooden ball on top of a stick one day just for practice, the ball slipped and fell on the back of my neck without hurting me in the least. It then at once occurred to me that if I could catch a ball by accident on the back of my neck without hurting myself, I ought to be able to do the same thing at any time I wanted to. So, I threw the ball up in the air, tried to catch it on the same place, did not quite succeed and was knocked senseless to the floor.

He said it had taken him a year to perfect the trick. It was one of his most audacious feats and astounded audiences around the world. The juggler considered it one of his most popular deeds, but not his most dangerous.

The second trick, which was demanded again and again, was the billiard table feat. Cinquevalli considered this one of his most difficult acts and it had taken eight years to perfect.

He came to the stage wearing a specially designed tunic that had several large pockets in various places. Then he balanced two billiard balls on the thick end of a cue, which was in turn poised on top of a third ball, which was balanced on a wine glass balanced on his forehead. With a flick of his body, the tower collapsed, and the three balls found their way into the pockets of the tunic. This was very popular during the 1909 tour of Australia.

In Sydney that year, Cinquevalli charmed large Tivoli audiences. He was accompanied on stage by his energetic and comical assistant Walter Burford. Burford had been with the juggler for ten years and knew every nuance of the act. His antics amused audiences and critics and featured in many reviews. Walter was often balanced in awkward positions by his boss and this added to the merriment of the juggler's turn.

They received a particularly warm reception in Sydney. On the first night, billiard balls travelled down one of Cinquevalli's arms across his chest to the other arm. They were balanced and manipulated in all manner of combinations. In another feat, which caused gasps of amazement, he used a pyramid triangle and a glass of water. The glass of water was placed on the base of the triangle, which was spun quickly on the tip of a cue above the head. Not a drop of water spilt to the stage.

Cinquevalli's speciality was juggling ordinary objects. He juggled paper, umbrellas, suitcases, walking sticks, glasses, billiard cues – the choice was endless.

His antics were described as 'mystifying and dazzling', and he was referred to as 'the great Paul Cinquevalli'. By the time of his third tour of Australia in 1909, his managers were asking him to refrain from introducing new material because audiences wanted the familiar billiard table and cannonball tricks and lined up to see them.

He performed before royalty in every country, entertained Queen Victoria, and King Edward VII, and was universally acclaimed as the 'world's greatest juggler'. He became so rich, he did not need to continue, but he could not retire. He tried, at least twice, but was miserable each time. He thrived on the thrill of performance and could not live happily without it.

His last trip to Australia was in 1914. However, his influence over Australian jugglers in the vaudeville era was immense, and every juggler who came after him, from 1899 onwards, was compared to the 'great Paul Cinquevalli'.

Cinquevalli was one of three highly skilled foreign jugglers who visited Australia in the early years of the twentieth century. The other two were Salerno and Kara. These two visited after Cinquevalli and suffered from comparison with him. Cinquevalli had conquered the hearts of Australians and it was almost impossible for other jugglers to compete.

Salerno

The German-born Salerno was widely recognised as one of the most technically skilled jugglers in the world when he arrived in Australia in January 1902, but this did not impress a Cinquevalli-mad Australia.

He was born in 1868 or 1869, and was a youthful practitioner of the art. He began juggling at the age of fifteen and was so addicted he ran away to pursue it against the wishes of his parents. They became reconciled to his decision when they realised he was making a large amount of money. Salerno said that 'I love my profession' and added, 'when I was younger, I worked so hard, I got the juggling disease', which meant that he 'couldn't do anything without juggling'. An indication of his obsession was the fact that he suffered seasickness on the trip to Australia but was more concerned with the lost practice time than the effect on his health.

Salerno was a more taciturn man than the gregarious and universally popular Cinquevalli and did not give undeserved praise. While Cinquevalli flattered Australia, Salerno was more critical, saying that he was unhappy with Melbourne's early lock-out laws, and comparing the city unfavourably with Europe. He also complained about the unavailability of juggling equipment, in particular India rubber balls, asking one interviewer, 'Where are your industries?' He eventually had to import his juggling props from Germany.

His act reflected his sober personality. Unlike Cinquevalli, Salerno was more formal, wearing a frock coat and bell topper hat on stage. While Cinquevalli was a showman who often dropped or pretended to drop onstage for dramatic effect, Salerno did not indulge in such tomfoolery. His juggling was precise and efficient.

He was often accused of copying Cinquevalli. However, many of the feats he performed were his own invention. He juggled everyday objects, including billiard balls, hats, umbrellas and cigars. He also had novelty lighted lamps which changed colour as he juggled them. Salerno was also working on a pen, ink and paper trick while touring Australia.

He was particularly adept with billiard cues. He juggled three, balanced one and threw a billiard ball atop the cue. He balanced two cues, and three balls, separated by chalk on his chin, and juggled three items in his hands simultaneously. In another trick, which showcased his contortionist skills, he held a glass in his mouth, took a bottle between his feet and raised them behind his back. He then emptied the contents of the bottle held in his feet, over his head and into the glass. In a departure from Cinquevalli, Salerno allowed audience members to examine his props, which proved his strength and dexterity.

He was well received in Australia, but towards the end of the tour he incorporated some extra bits of showiness into the act, suggesting it was not going as well as expected. The comparisons with Cinquevalli were constant and must have irritated a man who was as highly skilled.

Salerno stayed in Australia until May, and then a few months later, Cinquevalli returned and was greeted by enormous crowds. For the show, Cinquevalli had no peer, but for technical skill, Salerno was a master.

Kara

The third major international juggler to visit Australia during this time was Kara. He arrived in 1905 and toured the Tivoli Circuit.

Kara, born Michael Steiner, was a highly skilled German juggler who specialised in manipulating ordinary objects. Comparisons between him and Cinquevalli were constant during his Australian tour, but no victor was declared.

Kara's first performance in Sydney was in April 1905. It was notable for the acrobatic antics of his assistant, who was said to be better than Walter Burford. Kara also demonstrated some very skilled hat juggling, one of the earliest jugglers to do so in Australia.

His almost mystic manipulation of the top hat provokes genuine astonishment. The manner in which he twirls, catches and balances, one, two, three or more of these hats on his fingers, his ear, the tip of his nose or the end of his umbrella, is truly remarkable.

Kara also juggled everyday objects such as billiard balls, umbrellas and plates. He juggled a turnip and two knives, balancing the three at the end of the trick.

His assistant was a skilled acrobat and an essential part of the show. Kara would balance the assistant on his head, and they would perform tandem juggling tricks, passing objects from one to the other. At the end of the act, Kara would leave the stage, still balancing the assistant, head to head.

He was noted for his playfulness and desperation on stage. He often missed a trick and became annoyed, then he would try again and succeed to the delight of the audience. He, like Salerno, dressed formally on stage, every inch the gentleman in a dress coat and top hat.

In early May, in Sydney, the juggler fell ill with appendicitis and was hospitalised. He had an operation and was released, although he missed several dates. The illness affected his performance and although reviews were warm, he gave few interviews and spent time recovering. He remained in Australia until September, and then departed for England. He made a return visit in 1924.

The solo male juggler was very popular in the early years of the twentieth century, but the space was dominated by Cinquevalli, leaving little room for others to compete. To capitalise upon the success of Cinquevalli, many local jugglers began juggling with umbrellas and cannon balls, but the press complained that these acts were too similar and less skilful than Cinquevalli.

W.C. Fields

In 1903, Harry Rickards imported a comedy juggler, a man who spoke little on stage, but let his skill speak for him. His name was W.C. Fields.

Billed as an 'eccentric juggler', American Fields was twenty-three years old when he arrived in Australia, 'a comparatively good looking, fair coloured youngster…a good revolver shot and a capital horseman'.

Fields began his tour in Melbourne in June, travelled to Adelaide for a week in July and then had a two-month stint at the Tivoli in Sydney. His act was most notable for its comedy.

Fields dressed as a modern motorist, complete with goggles, said little, and let his antics and dumb show provide the laughs.

For a ten-minute turn in Adelaide, he used a battered, old grey bell topper hat and twisted it around his feet, hands and head. He then placed a cigar on the hat, put both on his toe and whipped them up so that the hat fell on his head and the cigar into his mouth. He followed this with three-ball juggling, using tennis balls. 'Under his control, the balls were made to bound from place to place with lightning speed.'

In Sydney and Melbourne, Fields did a billiard table trick. Using a trick pool table, he bounced balls off parts of his body, and they rebounded into the pockets of the table. He later performed this trick in movies, and it was hugely popular.

The juggler was very warmly received, particularly in Sydney, and demands for encores on his opening night were 'unreasonable'. The press praised his humour, saying that 'he does the most difficult feats with a drollness which is irresistibly funny'.

Fields returned to Australia in 1914 for another tour. He followed his juggling career with star turns on stage and with the Ziegfeld Follies in the United States. He gave up juggling eventually, partly because of his fondness for alcohol and partly because he wanted a more financially rewarding occupation. He found it in movies. Nonetheless, he gained his initial fame through juggling and was one of the most successful acts on the Tivoli stage in 1903.

The Women Jugglers

Juggling increased in popularity during the late nineteenth and early twentieth century and its rise coincided with the development of vaudeville and variety theatres around the world. The Australian theatrical experience echoed this.

Although juggling was, and still is, dominated by men, there were several very skilled and popular female jugglers who had successful tours of Australia. One woman took the top hatted male juggler trope and turned it into a uniquely feminine experience.

Rhodesia

'Beautiful', 'pretty' and 'ladylike', the 'lady Cinquevalli', Ma'mselle Florence Rhodesia, also known as Florence Smith, was one of the first female international jugglers to tour Australia. Florrie was born in 1885 in England, so she was a mere fifteen years old when she first came to Australia in 1900.

She made her debut touring Australia and New Zealand with Fitzgerald Brothers Circus and the brothers Fitzgerald, Tom and Dan, called her Rhoda.

In an interview, Rhoda said that she began her career in the circus at the age of eight as a slack wire walker. When her apprenticeship ended, she toured South Africa with Fillis Brothers and began juggling. While there, she met Cecil Rhodes and acquired the name Rhodesia. After returning to England, she began juggling on variety stages, where she was discovered by the Fitzgeralds and invited to Australia.

She toured for several years and her act incorporated several of Cinquevalli's tricks. Florrie turned herself into a billiard table and rolled balls around her body until they slipped into the pockets of a specially designed coat. She did 'everything Cinquevalli did'. Most contemporaneous accounts focused on her looks and ladylike demeanour, with one newspaper saying, 'the lady is personally very attractive which is a feature unto itself'. For a publicity shot in 1902, Rhoda wore male attire, including pants, a suit coat and a shirt. She also had a top hat by her side. This costume placed her firmly in the tradition of Kara and Salerno and contributed to her appeal, especially to male audiences.

Rhoda was well liked by her peers, and when she left Australia in 1903, she was given a cart full of flowers, serenaded by the music of the circus orchestra and presented with a gold medal from the Fitzgeralds. They also gave her a note.

Dear Rhoda, as you are now leaving Australia, we must express our sincere regret at your departure. You have behaved yourself always in a ladylike and graceful manner and you leave behind you many true friends and well-wishers. We consider you a true artist and a credit to your profession. – T and D.

According to a local newspaper, Rhodesia was the only lady juggler ever seen in 'these parts', referring to Australia and New Zealand. This was not quite true, as lady jugglers were occasionally seen in Australian circuses which toured New Zealand, but Rhoda was one of a kind, a woman performing a solo juggling act.

In 1905, Florrie wrote a letter to friends in Sydney announcing that she had married Mr William Seeley in Capetown, South Africa. Seeley had performed in Australia on the Tivoli Circuit as one of a team called Seeley and West. It is possible the pair met during Rhoda's tour.

Florrie with her husband returned to Australia in 1907 and performed at the Tivoli, but this time she was not well received. One newspaper dismissed her show, saying the only unique part was her gender. Time and imitators had apparently eroded her popularity.

She continued to perform with her husband, primarily in the United States. In 1910, the couple settled there and by the late 1920s Florrie was the proprietor of an inn in Suffolk, New York. Genealogical information suggests that she died around 1938 in the same area.

Kitty Harbeck

Only a few solo female jugglers toured Australia in the first decade of the twentieth century, but some were part of juggling pairs. One of these women was Kitty Harbeck, of the Harbecks.

Kitty was born in 1870 in Pennsylvania. By the time she was twenty-one, she was living with her husband, William A. Harbeck and working as a circus actor. William had trained as a contortionist, but one day he had a close encounter with a barrel that fell off a truck. The barrel split and a hickory hoop came spinning towards him. William caught it, spun it, and discovered a whole new career. He and Kitty became some of the first hoop spinners in the world.

They were working in London when Harry Rickards asked them to join the Tivoli in Australia. They arrived in 1902 and were a popular success, but the critics were not impressed, saying their act was 'not sensational'.

The Harbecks claimed to be the only people in the world who could spin seven or eight hoops on stage. They dressed in striking scarlet and gold outfits which highlighted Kitty's 'grace and good looks'. Their act consisted of rolling hoops around the stage, causing them to 'roll rapidly around themselves', then they 'threw hoops upon a slack rope which, striking the cord, returned along it to the performer who is holding one end between his teeth'. The couple performed the hoop tricks as a pair.

However, Kitty was also a juggler and a very talented one. As part of the show, she would walk on a slack wire balancing a lighted lamp on her head. Simultaneously she juggled four balls, four knives or four torches. Then she hopped off the wire and rejoined her husband to twirl more lighted hoops around the stage.

In Australia, William gave all the interviews and passed out photos of the couple. He stated that he had major shares in a mining company and owned his own nightclub. Kitty said little, but had a minor accident, spraining an ankle during a show. It was not serious, and she was soon performing again, walking on the wire, juggling, and twirling hoops around the stage.

They stayed in Australia for several months before returning to England. Although minor performers, they were engaged steadily for most of their lives and their marriage and partnership lasted until Kitty's death in 1936.

The second decade of the twentieth century saw an avalanche of overseas performers come to Australia, including two highly skilled female jugglers. Both were inspired by Cinquevalli and both brought their own peculiar talents to the juggling profession.

Lucy Gillett

Berlin-born Lucy Gillett arrived in Australia on 4 June 1913 for a four-month tour on the Tivoli Circuit. She was just eighteen years old and accompanied by her parents, Zelma and Fred. Both were 'dumb show' performers who retired from show business to support their daughter's career.

The family were based in England and Lucy performed in provincial English theatres as early as 1908, when she was thirteen. At fourteen, her father was reported for child cruelty because he was teaching his daughter juggling and acrobatics. He was not charged, and Lucy continued to practise. Lucy told the Australian press that she had been juggling since she was ten years old. It seems that her parents had long seen her as a path to a life of ease and affluence.

At eighteen, Lucy was 'a pretty girl, pleasantly plump and fair'. She was a modern woman, and was very interested in Zeppelins, longing for the days when everybody could travel on them. She had resented the long sea voyage to Australia because she could not practise juggling on a steamer.

Lucy was considered unique in vaudeville circles because of her high skill level and her gender. Her balancing and juggling were often compared favourably to her male peers, and in Adelaide they called her a 'Lady Cinquevalli'.

The Gilletts knew that Lucy's novelty was her gender, so they emphasised this in the show. Lucy's set was a kitchen and the props were domestic utensils and equipment including plates, chairs, tables, lamps,

and pot plants. The theme was Dutch Delft, and the colour scheme blue and white.

A typical performance began when the curtains parted to reveal Lucy sitting on a chair wearing a Dutch dress with long pantaloons. She then quickly blew out a lamp and began to juggle. She was a skilled foot juggler and alternated between using her feet and her hands to manipulate objects. She balanced a candle on her foot and threw it to her forehead, then she juggled three chairs. In a particularly clever trick, she perched a table on her forehead while juggling five balls in two hands and then in one. She then tossed the balls into receptacles sitting on the balanced table. The finale saw her balancing a table on two poles while on her back, letting it fall to her feet and then juggling it.

In Sydney, a wit in the audience almost caused her to drop. Lucy had a pot plant on her forehead, supported revolving plates with her mouth and was juggling other plates with her hands and holding a reading lamp on her left foot. This left her standing solely on her right foot. Suddenly a sarcastic young man in the audience yelled, 'What about your other foot, miss?' drawing much laughter from the audience and probably some angst from the young juggler.

Lucy was a very serious juggler. Those who met her said that 'she gives the impression that the only thing that matters on earth to her is juggling'. In Sydney, she arrived promptly on the Tivoli stage every day at ten a.m. for a two-hour practice session. She was passionately devoted to her craft and adamant that 'people who juggle cannot afford to be nervous'.

She performed in Sydney, Melbourne and Adelaide and left Australia in August 1913. Although she did not make a lasting impression on Australian audiences, her feats were incredible. There were several female jugglers at the time, but few displayed the skill level and artistic appeal of Lucy Gillett.

Selma Braatz

One who did, however, was Selma Braatz, who came to Australia the year after Lucy and was a protégé of Cinquevalli.

Selma was twenty-five years old when she set foot in Australia with her father, Fritz, and Clara, who was either her mother or aunt. She was a 'young and trimly built lady from Germany who juggled with any old thing in the way of light articles'. On stage, she wore a type of short suit, which was demure, but daring, as it revealed her legs.

Selma began her tour in January 1914, in Melbourne. The new year was pantomime season in the cities, so her appearance was not widely noticed. She appeared at the Tivoli in Sydney, but again was overshadowed by other events, in particular the introduction of the tango, the latest dance craze sweeping the nation. Selma, unusually for an international performer, also visited the countryside, travelling to Ballarat, a provincial town of Victoria, where she played in an open-air venue. She also visited Perth and Kalgoorlie, a mining town in Western Australia. Her itinerary suggested an adventurous spirit and a curious nature.

She balanced and juggled unusual household objects. She started by juggling a tennis racquet, then proceeded to use a bell topper hat and stick and manipulated both in strange ways that delighted the audience. She had difficulty with some of the balancing tricks in the open-air Britannia Theatre at Ballarat, with the wind being an uncontrollable factor which tended to blow things off their perch, but she had better luck with these feats in the bigger theatres of Melbourne and Sydney.

The act that won her most applause was balancing a tray, a wine glass, another tray and an egg on a billiard cue held upright on her chin. The trays were then knocked away and the egg fell into the wine glass without breaking.

As a finale, Selma juggled carriage lamps. The house lights were dimmed and as the lamps were thrown into the air, they became luminous, changing colour from white to red and on to violet. Selma was assisted on stage by Clara, who juggled soap bubbles. These were 'stiff bubbles [which] may be blown either from film cement or from a special soap solution, into the composition of which enters a little gum Arabic'. Apparently, Clara was the first person to juggle soap bubbles in Australia.

Selma and Cinquevalli were on good terms. They corresponded frequently and the great juggler called her 'Pauline', a reference to his own name, Paul. In Cinquevalli's mind, she really was 'the lady Cinquevalli'.

The Braatz family remained in Australia for several months and toured widely through the country. They returned overseas and continued juggling.

Selma died in New York in 1973 at the age of 89.

Club Juggling

Society in the first half of the twentieth century was changing quickly due to industrialisation and innovation. The first decade saw mass electricity available in Australia and Sydney's streets were electrically lit in 1904. Construction materials became more malleable and portable and motorised transportation was occasionally seen on the roads of Australian cities.

Juggling responded to these changes, and individuals in England and the United States developed new kinds of props. The juggling club was one of these.

The first person to juggle clubs on stage was an American called James DeWitt, who juggled Indian swinging clubs in 1885. Several other jugglers started to use Indian clubs in their act and by the 1890s jugglers such as Alburtus and Bartram, Derenda and Breen, and Morris Cronin had incorporated club juggling in their acts. By 1895, entrepreneur Edward Van Wyck was manufacturing colourfully decorated clubs for use on the stage.

There are several early references to club juggling in Australia. One of the first is by circus performer Marizles Wirth. Marizles was a prominent member of the Wirth Circus family who performed a juggling act on a horse. In 1893, she was on a boat travelling to South Africa when circus manager George Anderson introduced her to the India club. She started practising with it on board. The circus did not return to Australia until 1900 and Marizles allegedly juggled with clubs on horseback during her career.

Another early club juggler was John Pamplin, the minstrel performer. In 1899 he was 'club swinging and juggling' at the Theatre Royal in Adelaide. This is one of the earliest recorded performances of club juggling in a theatre in Australia.

Derenda and Breen

One of the first pair acts to pass clubs on an Australian stage was two Americans, Derenda and Breen, who carried Van Wyck clubs.

Derenda and Breen met at an Indian club swinging tournament in New York and from that meeting they developed a music hall act. They were the first club jugglers to incorporate comedy and patter in their performance, despite critics saying that club juggling was 'too pretty' for comedy.

They arrived in Australia in 1902. Their act was controversial, upset the local Indian club community, and caused a sensation.

Their show began when one of them leapt out of a life-sized poster at the back of the stage. Every night, a different juggler leapt from the backdrop, keeping audiences guessing which one was alive and which one was a picture.

They were comedians and made jokes as they dextrously juggled their clubs. They were pair jugglers and passed the clubs back and forth between themselves while standing in different positions. They tossed them back to back, over their heads, and then mounted a pedestal and exchanged eight clubs between them.

Derenda often had temper tantrums when the clubs misbehaved.

When Derenda made a miss, his rage became a thing awful to behold. Sometimes he would snap a mighty chain to pieces, sometimes with his teeth tear lumps from the top of a wooden pedestal.

The use of juggling clubs on stage led to a contest between club users in the country. Indian club swingers scoffed at the club jugglers, and the cultural space occupied by the club was contested between the athletes and the entertainers.

While Derenda and Breen were entertaining the crowd with their version of club juggling, well known axe and Indian club swinger Jack Harrison challenged them to a match. He called them 'fancy club swingers', a term of derision that insulted the art of juggling.

The animosity between the Indian club swinging community and the jugglers continued during the early 1900s. A club swinger wrote the following in a Queensland newspaper.

I am aware that the artistes 'on the boards' execute some marvellous and intricate evolutions, but their work savours more of jugglery than legitimate club swinging. As a rule, they use extremely light clubs, in fact were you to offer them ones weighing 3-4lbs they would be unable to do their wonderful finger swings catches and changes. This stage trick-club work looks very pretty and is indeed clever, but it does not bring any appreciable development, as the clubs being held with the fingertips confine the muscular work to the fingers, wrist and forearm.

The description of the club jugglers as 'artistes' who performed 'jugglery', often used as a synonym for trickery, dismissed the skills involved in juggling. The author clearly considered juggling inferior to club swinging. By 1910, this disdain of club juggling had spread, and Indian club swinging competitions were posting rules saying, 'no juggling allowed'. This indicated that club juggling was popular in the general community and was infecting the athletic halls of Australia.

The popularity of Derenda and Breen led to the arrival of several other imported club jugglers. Among them were Selbo, the Juggling Geraldos, and perhaps the most skilled and innovative club juggler in the world, Morris Cronin.

Selbo

Selbo's real name was David Horne and he was a Scottish juggler hired by Harry Rickards to tour Australia in 1907. He was the 'king of clubs'. His stage character was a young man dressed in casual sports clothes, his setting a tennis court, and in addition to juggling clubs, he also spun and juggled tennis racquets.

He was a dexterous club juggler but began his turn by juggling everyday objects. He walked upon the stage in his tennis clothes and hat, and proceeded to juggle the hat, a handkerchief, a cigarette and his tennis racquet. Then he juggled clubs, but not in a conventional fashion.

He juggled two clubs in one hand and removed his handkerchief to wipe his face, still juggling the clubs, then he removed his collar and tie and juggled the whole lot simultaneously. He also impressed the audience by reclothing himself while balancing a tennis racquet on his chin. He juggled three clubs and danced a cake walk while doing so. He also juggled plates and crockery in a skilful fashion.

He had a short tour but was among the earliest club jugglers on the Australian stage.

The Geraldos

The four Geraldos were brothers who juggled a whirlwind of clubs on the Tivoli stage in 1907. They were recruited from London by Harry Rickards and their act included hoop spinning and club passing.

They were unusual because of the large number of people passing clubs on stage. The curtain opened on three of the brothers standing in a triangle passing clubs from one to the other, flinging 'the twisting glittering things from one to the other with such speed and dexterity that they…dart about in the air like so many great hummingbirds'. Then, with no interruption to the pattern, a fourth Geraldo joined the throng, passing clubs and turning the glittering triangle into a sparkling square. Audiences were astounded by the number of people on stage, the whirling clubs and patterns produced by them. They were very popular.

Unfortunately, the career of the Geraldos was cut short by an earthquake in Italy in 1909. Two of the brothers disappeared and were never seen again after the disaster in Messina that year.

Morris Cronin

The most famous club juggler to visit Australia during the early twentieth century was Morris Cronin.

Cronin was born in the United States in 1869 and invented some innovative and popular three club juggling patterns, including throwing clubs under the legs (Albert throws) and juggling three clubs under the arms with one arm behind the back, known as contortion. These tricks are still performed by jugglers in the twenty-first century.

The juggler was a tall thin man with brown hair who had been juggling clubs on stage since the 1890s, making him one of the earliest exponents of the art. He was an innovative performer, a designer and maker of his own juggling clubs. He created his own illuminated clubs which he brought to Australia. He was also technically brilliant, with a strong stage presence and charismatic persona.

He walked on stage nonchalantly as 'grave as a judge' and dressed very formally. Then he began to juggle everyday items. Eventually, he juggled clubs as various assistants, dressed as waiters, walked on stage. Cronin threw the clubs at them, they dodged and weaved, caught them and threw them back. Towards the end of the club throwing, one of the assistants caught 'flying timber until he looks like a grotesquely decorated and mammoth porcupine'. The number of identically dressed waiters confused the audience, who liked to guess their number. To increase the drama and humour, Cronin was entirely silent throughout. The humour came from the antics of the assistants and their acrobatics as they navigated the flying objects.

Cronin's glowing clubs were featured in the finale. Their design was unique as they had light bulbs built into their structure. Cronin had patented the idea and it was a remarkable innovation for the time. The house lights were dimmed, and the theatre plunged into darkness as Cronin brought out these beautiful clubs. The 'elusive wil-o-the-wisp' lights made a dazzling display which mesmerised those who saw it.

Cronin was widely regarded as an expert technician and superb performer and his shows in Australia were warmly received. His success contributed towards the development of Australian club jugglers who sought to emulate his achievement.

International jugglers heavily influenced the development of Australian juggling. Their props were copied, their costumes duplicated, and their tricks practised. Some encouraged this. For example, Cinquevalli reportedly took time to teach local jugglers some of his tricks, others did not. The development of Australian juggling during the early twentieth century closely paralleled the arrivals of foreign visitors and their styles were duplicated by local performers who added a distinctive Australian twist to the juggling art.

The Australians

Juggling in Australia continually developed in the late nineteenth and early twentieth century and operated under the twin influences of the foreign visitors, particularly Cinquevalli, and the local circus community. These influences created new jugglers who at times surpassed their mentors and surprised the world.

From its earliest years, the circus in Australia included juggling. One of the major influences on early Australian juggling was the Ashton family. The Ashtons always included juggling as part of their circus, which started officially in 1851 when James Henry Ashton gained a licence in Tasmania. The circus became an institution that lasted through wars, depressions and catastrophes to become legendary. Ashton's hosted many jugglers, including Robert Taylor, Tasma and Rogers, and Ridgeway.

The Ashton family inspired later Australian jugglers with their shows, but they also trained many jugglers who later became internationally famous. Performers such as Arnold Jarvis, Harry Cameron, and the Wirth family, all trained with Ashton's circus.

Marizles Wirth

The Wirths eventually formed their own circus, but they were most famous for their role in adopting and training May Wirth, the internationally renowned equestrian. May's adoptive mother, Marizles Wirth, was a world-class performer in her own right. She walked the wire, she danced, she tumbled, she rode horses and she juggled.

Her father, John Wirth, originally came to Australia from Germany as a travelling musician. His sons, including Philip and George, also took up the profession. When Ashtons needed musicians, John took

the job, despite his dislike of circus. Eventually, all the boys worked at Ashtons off and on. They said that the Ashtons taught them circus skills and they taught the Ashtons music.

Marizles was born in Dalby, Queensland, in 1869. Her real name was Mary Elizabeth Wirth, but her nickname was 'Rill'.

She and her mother and siblings, including younger sister Madeleine, lived together, and moved together. She was educated at various schools, but her brothers and their circus adventures and misadventures dominated the rhythm of the household, particularly after the death of her father in her childhood. Marizles and Madeline went to school in Sydney and their early years were relatively normal despite the circus connection, with relatives coming and going and the girls learning common domestic tasks. However, that dramatically changed in 1880.

One day that year, Marizles and Madeline, aged eleven and eight respectively, were playing near Smith's Wharf (near current day Miller's Point) in Sydney, Madeline was lured into a store by a man and Marizles, hearing her screaming, raced to help. Both girls were indecently assaulted and were ill for some time afterwards. The man was later convicted and sent to prison for over ten years.

Marizles did not mention the incident in her diary, and neither of her brothers spoke of it in their memoirs, although it was reported in the press. Given this childhood trauma, the amazing accomplishments of both women were even more remarkable.

In 1885, Marizles's brother Philip had an accident and came to stay at the family home. When he recovered, her mother sent Marizles to join him in the travelling show. It was originally a three-month plan, but she never returned.

She started as a dancer, dancing the highland fling, but quickly started juggling. In Adelaide around 1886, she met Levarter Lee, who juggled on horseback. Soon Marizles was getting juggling 'things' made for her personal use.

Philip taught her to trick ride, and soon Marizles was juggling on a horse, with no saddle, bareback, as it galloped around the ring.

In August that year, she performed in Bendigo and Ballarat in Victoria. Dressed in a tight dress with puffy sleeves and short skirt, she jumped on a moving horse. Then as the horse galloped around the ring, Marizles, standing, juggled brass balls. Her next trick was to spin plates in one hand while simultaneously juggling balls in the other, still on the horse. She was deft and quick, and the act was tremendously popular

In 1888 in Newcastle, her act included 'knives' and 'rings' which she caught 'with the apparent ease of a terra firma conjurer while careering around the ring at a gallop'. She was so skilled that even a dangerously wet and muddy ring could not stop her. In 1891, she was described as 'daring 'and 'graceful' performing 'difficult' juggling tricks in Brisbane, on a muddy, cut-up track.

That year she married John Martin, a member of the circus, and in 1892 the couple had a daughter, Stella.

The depression of the early 1890s was tough for circus entertainment, crowds dwindled, and profits plummeted. In 1893, the family circus went on a world tour. They left for South Africa from Melbourne via boat, and during this journey, manager, George Anderson, taught Marizles to 'swing clubs'. This suggests that Marizles was one of the first Australian jugglers to use clubs.

The tour took her to South Africa, South America, Java and England. The circus returned to Australia in 1900 facing stiff competition from Fitzgerald Brothers.

When they returned to Australia, Marizles was an equal partner in the management of the circus and one of its star performers. She was advertised as the female Cinquevalli, and legend suggests that she juggled clubs on horseback. If so, this was one of the earliest public performances of club juggling in Australia.

In 1901, Marizles adopted a seven-year-old girl called May Zinga, who was quickly rechristened May Wirth. May became one of the most famous equestrian circus performers of all time. While May trained, Marizles performed. In 1906, her juggling act included 'balls, knives, fire arrows and rings' and was accompanied by a group of four clowns who added humour and spice to the turn. Little Miss May Martin, (May Wirth) was also in the show doing acrobatics.

In 1907, Marizles's husband died. Soon afterwards, she seems to have stopped the juggling act, replacing it with other equestrian feats such as a serpentine act, and in 1909 she was doing an artistic riding act with Edith Cooke.

However, by this time, May's astonishing abilities on horseback were being noticed by powerful people. In 1910, young May was somersaulting on a horse while it galloped around the ring. Her skills were brought to the attention of Ringling Brothers Circus in the United States and late that year the family received an offer from the most famous circus in the world.

In 1911, Marizles with Stella and May boarded a boat for San Francisco, and from that time her life was focused on May's career.

May became a superstar, but Marizles continually showed her intelligence and circus knowledge by guiding her daughter's career. She managed the family show, played ringmaster for the act, and kept them safe. In 1913, Marizles rescued May when her foot got entangled in a rope on a galloping horse. May was dragged around the ring several times and the ring hands could not free her. Marizles leapt into action and swiftly untangled May's foot, proving her bravery, and possibly saving her life.

She guided the family around the world travelling to Europe and finally settling in the United States. In 1930 she was living in New York with Stella, May, and their husbands.

Marizles died there in 1948, aged seventy-eight.

The Lentons

There were other Australians who practised juggling in the early 1890s. Two of them were the Lenton brothers, who incorporated a hat juggling routine into their acrobatic act.

Frank and John Lenton were typical of performers who transformed the focus of their act towards juggling after Cinquevalli performed in Sydney. Before that, they were primarily acrobats and balancers.

They claimed to be from Geelong in Victoria. John was born in 1856 and Frank, whose real name was Francis Carr, a year later. When they were eight and nine years old, they were apprenticed, adopted or sold to an acrobatic troupe led by Thomas Lenton. In that era, unwanted children were often unofficially 'adopted' by itinerant troupes as there was little regulation over children and their welfare. Thomas Lenton was one of the men who brought the Dragon Japanese Juggling Troupe to Australia in 1867 and reports about the tour mention a pair of juvenile acrobat brothers called Frank and Johnny who did their master 'great credit' with their tumbling

In 1895, they returned to Australia after many years touring the world and they performed as a pairs act at a benefit show for Myra Kemble in 1896 at the Lyceum in Sydney. They were billed as 'The Lenton Brothers' and gave an exhibition of 'Marvellous hat throwing and head to head balancing' while dressed in long flowing Chinese garb.

At the time, hat throwing involved tossing hats with rubber rims, from one person to another. The hats were thrown like frisbees, and the heavier rims ensured steady flight. The Lentons also did simple hat juggling tricks like tossing a hat from foot to head.

The Lentons returned from another long world tour in 1902 and were billed as acrobats, comedians and hat jugglers, and they had added another member, Frank's wife, Kitty Lenton.

The brothers were some of the first people to manipulate hats on an Australian stage. In 1902, the act consisted of acrobatic feats including a finale of balancing on top of each other head to head upon a slanted piano.

In terms of juggling, their hat manipulations were different to current day hat juggling. The brothers used straw hats, which they threw from one head to another, but their most outstanding trick was 'the spinning of hats from the circle of the theatre across onto the stage where they were caught on the head of one of the brothers'. It was a highly original, amusing and delightful act according to New Zealand reviewers.

The Lentons had a long career in Australia and the act had several incarnations. In 1905, Kitty and Frank had a dispute about marital maintenance that reached the courts. Frank accused Kitty of having an affair with well-known theatrical manager Ben Fuller who she was working for as a solo act. Frank then tried to extort Kitty, and said that he would divorce her, presumably so she could stay with Fuller, if he was paid £500. Kitty disputed the alleged affair and stated that Frank was not supporting her financially. She also accused him of writing to several theatrical managers, threatening to sue them if they employed her under the name of Lenton.

These disputes led to the act splitting. John had already left and had been replaced by a man called Ronald Maloney, who later teamed with his wife Ruby to form the Tossing Testros, another juggling group.

The group continued for several years, and a Lenton trio was billed as throwing and juggling hats up to the beginning of the First World War, when they disappear from theatrical bills.

Mishaps and Misdeeds

It was Cinquevalli who made juggling popular and this popularity extended to the public spaces and private homes of Australia. Shortly after his first tour in 1899, juggling became a more common sight on the streets of the cities and towns and more itinerant jugglers toured the countryside begging for food or money.

Several juggling mishaps and misdeeds were reported in the newspapers in the early twentieth century which suggests that juggling was spreading among the general population. It seems that juggling was becoming more widely seen, talked about and practised in the country.

In 1902, young Arthur Dykes was showing off to his friends by juggling three coins. He aimed to catch all three in his mouth as a grand finale to his impromptu show. He threw three into the air and caught the first successfully, but unfortunately it slid down his throat. He was taken to hospital, but the coin could not be extracted or even located by X-ray. Arthur was not disturbed. He was happy, he said, 'to have money in him'. It was presumed that the coin would eventually pass through him with no ill effects.

Two years later, jugglers were once again in the newspapers, but this time allegedly involved in criminal activity.

Sydney was home to several itinerant jugglers at the time. In late 1903, a young cockney juggler, going by the name of 'Smith', had been amusing lunchtime crowds in the city with 'chair balancing, plate spinning and ball tossing' for several months. In February, the next year he was charged with stealing a handbag. This was apparently a ruse by the authorities, who wanted him on another charge. Young Smith had been involved with a young lady who subsequently got pregnant. She was almost due to give birth and, as the date grew closer, Smith ran further away. He had attempted to sign on as a seaman to avoid his responsibilities, but the authorities had been warned and he was charged with theft to stop his escape. He was ordered to pay ten shillings and sixpence a week to the lady and the charge of theft was dropped.

However, theft and pickpocketing were rampant in Sydney and often associated with street juggling. In September 1904, a crowd gathered on the corner of Park and George Streets to watch a juggler perform on a Saturday night. Among the crowd was a retired army man Daniel O'Flanagan from Waverly. Daniel watched the performance and as he walked away from the crowd noticed that his watch and chain were missing. He scanned the people around him and noticed nineteen-year-old Thomas Murphy acting suspiciously. O'Flanagan immediately tried to grab Murphy, who hit the older man in the face, knocking his hat off. Murphy was arrested, charged and convicted of assault, but O'Flanagan never got his watch back.

Another theft was associated with, perhaps, the same juggler, who this time was performing on Moore Street between Pitt and Castlereagh Streets in the city. It was November, hot and dry, and a crowd of fifty to sixty people was watching the juggler perform at lunchtime. A man was seen to be 'working the crowd', pickpocketing them, and a nearby policeman arrested Walter Cook for theft. Walter, who claimed to be the son of a man of 'independent means', denied the charges. He said he was waiting to meet his father for lunch and watching the show to pass the time. After giving the juggler a 'couple of coppers', he was arrested. A jury found Walter not guilty and, again, the missing items were never found.

The situation of children in the early twentieth century was not as well defined legally as it would become and it was common for circus troupes and travelling entertainers to 'adopt' or 'buy' unwanted children, train them and profit from them. May Wirth, who was adopted by Marizles, was a prime example. However, sometimes, parents were not so eager to lose their children.

Jim Kenny and Billy Dalton were two eleven-year-old boys from

Newtown, a suburb near Sydney. Both went to Erskineville Public School nearby. One day, instead of going to confirmation class, they idled in University Park and saw two men camping there. The men were juggling knives and performing acrobatics, and the boys were mesmerised. The jugglers told Jim and Billy that they would be great tumblers, and that intrigued the youngsters. Later that day, the boys again saw the men, Richard Hefrand and Henry Wilson, as they were preparing to leave the city. Jim and Billy were devastated, and on impulse asked if they could travel with the jugglers. The men shrugged and agreed. The four tramped all the way to Mudgee, a town over the Blue Mountains. They begged for food by performing acrobatic tricks, but the boys did not enjoy the itinerant lifestyle.

The Kenny and Dalton families reported their sons missing, and Hefrand and Wilson were arrested for abduction when they reached Mudgee and sent to Newtown to face court. The charges regarding Jim Kenny were dropped almost immediately, because Jim stated that he had willingly joined the men. The Dalton case resulted in the men being acquitted, because Billy too, said he had left voluntarily.

The happy result for Hefrand and Wilson was that they could continue their itinerant tumbling and juggling careers. Billy and Jim, on the other hand, were forever banned from the circus life.

The Australian Vaudeville Jugglers

Many aspiring Australian jugglers were trained by the Ashton family, who willingly passed their knowledge to the younger generation. Often, children who had seen Cinquevalli sought out the Ashtons for training, and upon reaching adulthood became seriously dedicated to the art.

Arnold Jarvis (Arnoldi)

One of these people was Arnold Jarvis. Arnold Jarvis was born in South Australia in 1881 and trained with one of the Ashtons from the age of sixteen for two years. At the same time, he was studying drawing with artist Hans Heysen, and he combined his two skills to produce a surprising vaudeville act.

As a young man, Jarvis's main ambition was to juggle on stage, which did not please his parents. However, in 1901, his wish became reality and he juggled on the Tivoli Circuit, where he was billed as the 'Australian Cinquevalli'.

It is clear from his notebooks that Arnold was influenced by, and probably had seen, Cinquevalli. They contain drawings of a figure juggling an umbrella, a hat and another item, another of a trick with a plate and umbrella, and illustrations demonstrating the billiard ball trick complete with pockets in the tunic.

Arnold, billed as Arnoldi, juggled three and four balls under his legs and behind his back while balancing a billiard ball on a cue. He also performed Cinquevalli's billiard ball trick, where the juggler would manipulate billiard balls around his body to have them eventually fall into a specially designed coat that he wore on stage.

Jarvis had other tricks too. He juggled a silk hat, an umbrella and cigar, ending with the hat on his head, the cigar in his mouth and the

umbrella in his hand. He also tossed a half-crown from his toe to his eye and strutted around the stage like an elderly gentleman. The young man claimed that his feats were original, but he was generally regarded as a skilful imitator who performed with sharpness and accuracy. One original and surprising feature of his act was a demonstration of his artistic skills. He did lightning sketches, and in Western Australia, painted a detailed landscape in oils in three minutes and gave it to the audience.

In 1902, the twenty-one-year-old Arnold Jarvis married a soubrette, Frederica, on the Tivoli stage. They remained married for several years. However, Arnold was already showing signs of the alcoholism which would haunt most of his life. He was very ill with the disease and was sent to a succession of homes and institutions, and by 1911 he had disappeared from the theatre and from Frederica's life.

That year, Frederica sued for divorce because Arnold had failed to support her and their son. As a result, she claimed they were living in poverty. The court ordered a search and Arnold was eventually discovered in Ballarat, where he was served the divorce papers.

Arnold Jarvis remarried and in later life pursued a career as a landscape artist. His paintings are still sold today. He died in 1959, and is remembered by his descendants, who treasure his art, as a gentle, respectable man who loved life and nature.

Anglo the Juggler

Another young Australian juggler had problems with his wife. However, he solved them in a very violent way.

Rundle Street in Adelaide was a popular place for young men and women to walk and socialise on Saturday nights in 1904, but in February that year a tragedy terrified the crowds.

Florence Horton, aged twenty-two, was walking down the street with two friends when she was approached by her husband, Tom, who beckoned her away for a private conversation. Her girlfriends were afraid of Tom and held Florence back. They knew he could be violent. Tom, rebuffed, walked away, but suddenly he turned round, took a revolver from his pocket, and shot Florence three times in the back. She stumbled a few steps and collapsed into the arms of a nearby constable. Amid the screams and turmoil, Tom ran away, while Florence died in the street. The police found Tom in the Adelaide Hills a few days later and arrested him for his wife's murder.

Thomas Horton was a juggler.

Born in Adelaide in 1879, young Thomas was the only surviving child of five born to his mother. His father died in an asylum when he was young. Thomas once fell out of a tree when he was a child, but it was an attack in London, according to his mother, that led to a stutter in his speech and a nervous manner. In his local neighbourhood, Tom was known as 'cranky Tom' or 'silly Tom' and there were rumours he was illiterate.

The year before the murder, Tom travelled to London and while there visited the offices of *London Magic* magazine, where he introduced himself as 'Professor Anglo, Australia's greatest juggler and equilibrist'. However, Tom's career in Australia did not live up to his billing.

In 1902, he reached the pinnacle of his fame with a six-night contract at the Tivoli Theatre in Adelaide. He was described as an accomplished juggler and balancer of 'neatness and precision' who practised 'double balancing' and performed 'four or five movements' with 'ease and grace'. Thomas was warmly applauded at the Tivoli.

He was also, allegedly, the author of a book about juggling called *The Art of Modern Juggling*, which he published when in London. The book describes in detail how to juggle balls and clubs, and balance umbrellas, hats and other household items. It is a manual of early twentieth-century juggling and heavily influenced by Cinquevalli, perhaps suggesting that Thomas had seen the master at work. The author asserts that a juggler must live the life of a 'trained athlete, sacrificing everything to his profession'. Practice and patience were the keys to good juggling performance, according to Anglo.

Unfortunately, Thomas's marriage to Florence Lovell, which happened in 1903, was very unhappy. It was his second marriage. His first wife, who he married when twenty-one, had died leaving him with three children. Florence had a child herself, and the crowded household was a scene of poverty, confrontation and violence.

He was a jealous husband who constantly accused Florence of infidelity and suspected that she was working as a prostitute because she had a sexually transmitted disease. Thomas's paranoia reached a crescendo after Florence left him and the result was the murder on Rundle Street.

Thomas Horton, aka Anglo the juggler, was hanged in Adelaide Gaol in May 1904 for the crime of murder. Some experts believed he was not culpable due to psychological instability, but this defence was dismissed at trial. Tom expressed regret before his death and wrote five or six letters to relatives and friends, but the chaplain who accompanied him to the gallows believed he had no morality and no knowledge of the scriptures. This did not prevent his death from being instantaneous.

Lennon, Hyman and Lennon

The success of Derenda and Breen and their club passing act in 1902 led to the rise of local imitators and innovators. One famous Australian group of club passers was Lennon, Hyman and Lennon.

They were known individually as Albert (Bert) Lennon, Edward (Ted) Lennon and Frank Hyman. The three began their career as acro-

bats and began club juggling as a group to capitalise upon the growing popularity of the art. This eventually led to the formation of their own theatre circuit.

The most famous of the three was Bert Lennon, who was a Sydney man born in the 1870s. He and Edward Lennon began as the Lennon Brothers and worked in an amateur group called the Electric Minstrels in inner Sydney during the mid-1890s.

After this start, they toured Australia with a troupe led by Irving Sayles. Irving was a very famous African American performer who had starred on the Tivoli Circuit. He had good connections and was well regarded in the industry. It was at this time that the Lennons met Frank Hyman, a contortionist, and formed a trio. They mostly did acrobatics and comedy skits. There is no record of them juggling at this time.

They toured New Zealand in 1900 with Dix's Gaiety Company and in 1901 performed a 'Demons and Frogs' dance which was noted in the press.

In 1902, the three left Australia for England. While there, they performed a comedy skit called 'Heroes of the Australian Bush', which featured two Aboriginal characters and a miner. It was a hit with London audiences and led to a two-year tour of the country.

In 1904, they returned to Australia with a two-part act. The first was an acrobatic song and dance and the second, a club passing act. Somewhere in England, the three had acquired some juggling clubs and juggling skill, and they brought them home.

Their success with the juggling part of the show led to an engagement with William Anderson in 1906. They starred as a major part of his pantomime *Sinbad the Sailor* that year. The role focused on their club passing act and featured Hyman as a dummy clown. In advertising they juggled nine clubs, the Lennon brothers wore all-white clothing and Hyman, in a striped shirt, stood between them.

Their act was a high-energy club passing extravaganza.

A display of juggling with Indian clubs which they handled with remarkable proficiency, exchanging flying clubs with one another, and sometimes surrendering three clubs in mid-air with an air of perfect nonchalance.

They performed with speed and dexterity and were so fast that the clubs seemed like a blur in the air. Newspapers described their manipulations as 'astounding'. The finale was a skilful exchange of nine clubs between the three men which 'created the greatest enthusiasm'.

After the pantomime, the three formed their own vaudeville troupe which included their wives. The Lennon, Hyman and Lennon troupe toured the provincial areas of Australia, including Rockhampton, the Darling Downs, Lismore and Mackay.

Bert was the most prominent of the three, and summarised their belief in Australian performers in an interview in 1909, saying that 'In Adelaide, you get a better all-round vaudeville show than you will see in the London Halls.' By 1910, they had earned enough to settle in one place and chose Adelaide. They invested in their own theatre, the Empire, where they turned their belief into practical action and produced vaudeville shows featuring local entertainers.

They were in a partnership for many years. However, after the war, references to Ted and Frank are scarce. Bert remained a prominent figure in the Adelaide entertainment industry and community until his death in 1954.

The Exports

Several Australian jugglers served apprenticeships with Ashtons, had stage experience on the Tivoli Circuit in the early 1900s and were influenced or inspired by Cinquevalli. Many of them eventually found better opportunities overseas and developed long and successful international careers. Some of the outstanding examples of Australians who conquered the world were Stan Kavanagh, Harry Cameron, Victor Martyn and Maud Florence.

Stan Kavanagh

One Australian juggler gained worldwide fame with his comedy juggling. He was a Victorian and started his long career in the variety halls of Sydney Australia with his brother, Frank. His name was Stan Kavanagh.

Frank and Stan were born in Victoria, Frank in 1887, and Stan, as Arthur Stanislaus Kavanagh, in 1889. Their father was a bank manager, and according to legend, the boys had seen a juggler in a circus and became intrigued.

They were sent to boarding school in Sydney, a reputable one, called St Josephs, at Hunters Hill. It was a Catholic school, which suggests that the family was Irish Catholic, a suggestion further reinforced from Frank's Irish letter in 1914 highlighting the Home Rule debate.

In 1907, a Kavanagh juvenile started juggling on stage in some of the lesser variety halls in Sydney. This was most likely Frank, as Stan may still have been at school. The next year, a duo, the Kavanagh Boys, appeared.

In May 1908, the Kavanagh boys were travelling with the Sayers company in regional areas of Australia. That month, they were in Broken Hill, a mining town in the far west of New South Wales. At the Crystal Palace, they competed in a juggling competition against the

pair of Walker and Sturm. The competition was judged by a committee of citizens and based on comedy, style, dexterity and attractiveness. The Kavanaghs lost the money on offer by a vote of nine to two.

Later that year, their experience with the smaller company paid off when they were engaged at the National Amphitheatre on the Brennan Circuit. This was the second vaudeville circuit in Australia, the first being the Tivoli, and was a major step up for the brothers.

Their routine involved club and hoop juggling. They had a clever bit where they each juggled three clubs back to back and caught them end upon end. Their hoop juggling involved getting the hoops to recoil back to the jugglers on the stage. It was not a novel routine, but they had some unique club manipulations, and showed 'ingenuity' and 're- markable' feats.

After their short stop in the big time, the brothers were engaged on an overseas tour by Harmston's Oriental Circus. It was a three-year tour of Asia and included China, Japan, Java, Malaya, Cambodia, Korea and the Philippines. According to Frank, the weather was hot and the work long. They worked seven days a week, including Sundays, one night show and two matinees. It was also expensive, so Frank and Stan supplemented their pay by doing private performances. Frank later said that illness was not much of a problem with Harmston, with only two performers dying in the previous twenty years.

The young men became homesick and returned to Australia in 1911. Upon arrival, they gained a private audition with Harry Rickards and were engaged on the Tivoli Circuit. A major leap forward for their career.

At the Tivoli, they juggled and spun tennis racquets and clubs. Their act was described as 'nimble' and 'unerring' and warmly received. In Sydney, they employed a 'strange looking dummy' to provide humour and a 'ripple of amusement' ran through the audience at their antics.

In June, Frank married Agnes Fanning, from Sydney. The wedding was a prominent affair and discussed in the social pages. Stan was one of the groomsmen and the presents were quite lavish. The couple travelled by motor car to a honeymoon spot in Medlow Baths, in the Blue Mountains west of Sydney.

In October, after about nine months' continuous work, the pair decided to travel to London to try their luck. Frank fortunately was a natural gossip and wrote regularly to Australian newspaper friends about their travels around the world

In 1913, he described their South African experience saying that 'South Africa cannot be compared to Australia as a show country'. He complained it was expensive, the engagements were short, only a week-long, and the train travel long.

In 1914, they were in Belfast, where 'great excitement prevails… over the Home Rule Bill'. By 1915, they were in England, 'where the general lament is that no booking is being done ahead, the war threw hundreds of artists out of work'. He added that at one point he and Stan were billed as Austrians rather than Australians and had to alert the newspapers that they were not in fact enemy spies. That year, Stan married Henrietta Richards in Newcastle, and Frank alerted his Australian friends to the happy news.

By 1915, Frank was tired of the constant touring and made plans to return to Australia. He had waited to ensure that the Kavanagh name was well established before leaving, and Stan's marriage seems to have convinced him it was time to go home. The war delayed the parting, but in 1916, Frank returned to Australia, leaving Stan and Henrietta and another juggler, to continue the act in England.

From 1918 to 1920, Stan and his troupe toured England, appearing in provincial and London Theatres. In 1922, Stan supported famous Scottish comedian Harry Lauder in London and continued the engagement in Australia in 1923.

In Australia, Stan performed a comedy juggling routine for Lauder. He manipulated bell topper hats, tennis balls and India rubber clubs in a routine that was described as 'dexterous' and 'excellent'. He had an assistant, probably Henrietta, and was quiet throughout the act. One newspaper said that they 'had no idea that modern juggling had come so near to the standard of the late juggling genius Cinquevalli' until they saw Stan, and that his turn was worth the price of admission alone.

Stan remained in Australia after Lauder left and performed as a solo juggling act until late 1923. He was asking £60 a week for his shows but could not come to an agreement with any employer. He decided to go to the United States with his wife Henrietta and two daughters, Olive and Joan, and they arrived in San Francisco in January 1924. Shortly afterwards, he made an application to become a naturalised US citizen.

Stan's career in the United States skyrocketed until twenty years later he was being called America's best juggler. He started with the Keith circuit and was a hit. He continued juggling regularly on stage and occasionally in movies. In 1937, he appeared in a six-minute silent juggling comedy routine in 'the Big Broadcast of 1937'. That same year he appeared in the Ziegfeld Follies with Gypsie Rose Lee and Fanny Brice at the Wintergarden on Broadway.

Stan acquired a nickname, 'Kavy', during the 1930s and in the Second World War participated in a USO tour in the Pacific which included Australia. It was his first visit in twenty years. He said that Sydney had changed a lot and in an interview refused to be drawn into a comparison between the women of Australia and America.

A video of Stan juggling, which seems to be from this period, shows him with a Charlie Chaplin moustache. He is lightning quick, juggling three balls almost too fast for the camera to catch. He is smiling and clearly still enjoying his work.

In 1951, an Australian newspaper reported that Stan had died in England after going there to recover from an illness. This brief note was the only obituary in Australian newspapers for a man who had brought Australian juggling to the world.

Maud Florence and Victor Martyn

Two other Tivoli graduates became well known overseas and they had children who continued the family juggling tradition. Maud Florence and Victor Martyn are best known for being the parents of 'Topper' Martyn, a famous international juggler and magician. However, before 'Topper' was born, his parents had a colourful career in Australia.

Maud Florence was born Mary Maud Thyer in Queensland on 22 July 1887. She was one of a large family and the daughter of a budding theatrical entrepreneur, Charles Thyer.

Maud was six years old when she started performing. She, her brother George, and sister Ada were the Thyer trio, child acrobats and contortionists.

In March 1894, they performed at the Royal in Brisbane and in early December they performed at the Gaiety in the same city. Later that month, they appeared in Sydney as part of the annual pantomime, *Cinderella*, and the *Sydney Telegraph* called them an act of 'considerable merit'.

The Williamson pantomime was a yearly tradition in Australia. That year it started at Christmas in Sydney then travelled to Perth, went to Melbourne for Easter 1895, and arrived in Brisbane, Queensland, in May. It was an extravagant production with beautiful handmade sets and scores of ballet girls and children who filled the stage with dancing, singing and acrobatic feats.

In Brisbane, a member of the Society of Prevention of Cruelty went to see *Cinderella* and was horrified to see the very young Thyer children performing at ten thirty at night. They immediately wrote to the management protesting this abuse and referred to the law in Britain which prevented child labour. They also pointed out that Queensland was in the process of passing a similar law.

J.C. Williamsons was the premier legitimate theatre company in the colony. They prided themselves on providing high-lass entertainment, so the complaint was taken seriously. Williamson management blamed Charles Thyer, who had made the contract. The manager said that because Charles was a Queenslander, they assumed he knew the law. The Thyer act was immediately terminated and the family lost a very lucrative source of income.

Of course, that did not stop them performing. In January 1897, they were on the vaudeville circuit performing at the Gaiety in Brisbane, and in February they appeared at the Theatre Royal 'tumbling, balancing and posturing'.

By 1899, the family had changed their name to the more exotic Les Thieres and now consisted of five members, including Maud. She was also appearing as Maud Thyer and singing songs such as 'I want one like Pa had'.

Shortly afterwards, Les Thieres incorporated bicycle stunts, such as bicycle polo, into their act. In 1901, they were engaged by the Tivoli Theatre Circuit travelling to Melbourne and Sydney, Maud may also have sung during this tour, doubling the money for the family.

Maud was a person of many talents, dancer, singer, acrobat, cyclist and contortionist, and it seems equally clear that she was destined to have a solo career. In 1906, she started appearing alone at the Tivoli as a singer, acrobat and clog dancer. According to her son, one of Maud's specialties was donning ice skates and dancing on a marble table eliciting sparks which lit up in time to the music. The Tivoli was the most prestigious variety/vaudeville circuit in the country and Maud, although not a headliner, was a regular for almost four years. This meant that she had a reliable and probably well-paid position which was highly unusual in such an unstable industry. She was occasionally mentioned in gossip columns, one saying that she was writing songs, and was well known by audiences and critics.

However, after 1910, Maud stopped being a solo act and became part of a duo. She had met future husband, Victor Martyn, and juggling became her newest accomplishment.

Victor was born to Alexander and Eliza Martin in Hotham in Victoria in 1885. According to his son Topper, Victor learnt juggling from Harry Cameron, later known as the Great Carmo. As a youngster, Harry taught himself juggling after being inspired by a Cinquevalli performance and swapped his skills for Victor's magic skills.

At the age of twenty, Victor was juggling for local events such as the local football club. In 1905, he amused them with juggling and other tricks. His balancing and juggling of balls were very good and he performed with 'ease and pleasantness'. The next year, he was juggling for the local state school.

Victor turned twenty-one in 1906 and therefore was legally an adult. From 1907, he started juggling in travelling troupes and theatres as part of the duo Jarvis and Martyn.

Frank Jarvis had come to Australia in 1906 as part of the Bostock and Wombwell circus. He was partnered with another juggler called Campbell, but in mid-1907 the pair split. Victor took Campbell's place in the act.

Victor and Jarvis initially worked for the Brennan Circuit, the second-tier vaudeville circuit in Australia. Then in 1908 they hit the big time and worked for Harry Rickards and the Tivoli in Western Australia. Their act combined juggling and comedy. They spun hoops, and 'performed astonishing feats with tennis balls, racquets, plates, clubs, lighted torches and numerous other utensils'. One of the other acts in the show was a young acrobat and singer called Maud Florence, who was told by a local newspaper that doing the 'splits' was barbarous.

Jarvis and Martyn stayed with the Tivoli for a short time. At the end of 1908, the pair travelled to Canada and toured the United States. Maud remained in Australia but split from the Tivoli Circuit in 1909 and began performing with Brennan.

Victor returned to Australia in 1910 and that year in Melbourne, Victor and Maud married. Maud listed her place of usual residence as the Tivoli Theatre in Sydney.

Soon they were juggling as a duo. According to Topper, Maud had learnt juggling directly from Cinquevalli. This is possible as Cinquevalli always performed for the Tivoli Circuit during his tours of Australia and one of those tours was in 1901 when Maud was also performing at the Tivoli.

In November 1910, they played at the Star Court in Brisbane. Maud sang some songs, including 'I'll do anything in the World for you', and she and Victor did a 'double turn' with balls and clubs. Then Victor performed as a solo juggler. He juggled and balanced cigar boxes, washing tubs, buggy whips, plates, balls and lighted clubs, and was the hit of the evening. Victor and Maud shared the performance with a novelty, Pathé pictures, which showed world events on a movie screen. It was one of the early signs that live theatre's role as the sole source of entertainment was about to be challenged by the new moving pictures technology.

In 1911, Victor performed a solo juggling act at the National Amphitheatre in Sydney. Meanwhile, Maud was preparing for the birth of their first child Decima, who was born in Sydney that year. After she recovered, the family of three hit the road travelling to regional Queensland in 1912, where they played as part of a show with moving pictures. Victor was called 'a juggler of unquestionable merit and the highest ability'.

However, their opportunities in Australia were limited, so they decided to travel. In October 1912, they packed up and headed to the United States, where they performed as a juggling duo for some time. By the 1920s, they had established themselves as consistent and regular performers in England where they performed a sketch called 'the Tennis Court.' In 1923, Maud had their second child, Victor junior, later known as Topper, who became a world-famous magician and juggler.

The family visited Australia in 1929 and toured the Tivoli Circuit in Melbourne and Sydney as Martyn, Florence and Martyn. Eighteen-year-old Decima had joined the act. It was the Depression era and Australian theatres were combining vaudeville acts with the new novelty sensation the talkies. The juggling family appeared in the second half of the show with a line-up of comedians and sketch artists. Their act was described as 'a startingly intricate display of juggling'.

During the tour, Victor gave an interview to a sports newspaper where he discussed his 'system' of horse betting. Victor combined his knowledge of form with astrology to guide his bets. He informed the paper that he thought his system was ninety-eight per cent accurate at predicting winners.

It was a short tour, and the family returned to England later that year.

Maud and Victor continued juggling and as their children grew older, they started their own acts. Decima had a long career as a juggler partnering with her husband Jack Cooke, a member of the famous Cooke circus family. Topper became a juggling and magic superstar. He performed all his life and was known for juggling on ice skates and producing several books on comedy magic.

Victor Martyn died in 1961 in England, while Maud died in 1967, also in England.

The Great Carmo

Another internationally famous Australian performer and Tivoli graduate was Victor's juggling tutor, Harry Cameron, also known as the Great Carmo.

Harry Cameron – his friends called him Jack – was born in Victoria in 1881. His family were respectable Scots who had emigrated to Australia, but Harry was a curious boy and one day, after seeing Cinquevalli, he was inspired to become a juggler.

He practised juggling and Cinquevalli-like balancing even while apprenticed to a grocer and a brass foundry, and apparently during this time, he met Victor Martyn and taught him some juggling skills.

The life of an apprentice, be it to a grocer or a metal worker, did not appeal to Harry and he started to clandestinely perform in local minstrel shows. When his family discovered his extracurricular activities, they threw him out and Harry began the life of a travelling entertainer.

He apparently worked with Ashton's Circus for a while and learnt some acrobatics and tumbling and juggling tricks there. According to legend, he had a fall from a high wire and this injury reunited him with his family. Interestingly, Cinquevalli had a similar story about falling from a trapeze when a youngster, which led to him becoming a juggler.

It is not until 1901 that the first mentions of Carmo the juggler appear in the newspapers. He was twenty years old and performing with Rowley's Waxworks.

The Waxworks were a travelling show that visited regional and city areas around Australia. In 1901, it had figures of Queen Victoria, Gladstone, Charles Dickens and Shakespeare. It also had lifelike waxes of prominent criminals. The show included a small variety performance which included a Punch and Judy show, a singer, a gymnast, a comedian and a juggler, Carmo, who were all 'well received'.

In November 1901, Fuller's Empire Vaudeville Company introduced to Sydney, Carmo, 'who does wonderful contortion feats while juggling.' From that date, Carmo toured the vaudeville circuits in regional Australia as a juggler and balancer.

In 1902, Carmo, or Kharmo, played the Gaiety Theatre in Sydney and he balanced the four legs of a heavy table on four billiard cues, the tips of which rested in a leather cup which he gripped in his teeth. A review called it 'A feat truly'.

In 1903 in Brisbane, he carried a table with a young man on it, on a stick balanced on his chin, and drank a glass of wine (without hands) while balancing a lighted lamp on his head. That year in Sydney he married Nellie Lloyd, who joined his act as an assistant.

In 1904, Mr and Mrs Cameron appeared as the Carmos in Hobart, Tasmania, and did a tour of New Zealand with Fuller's entertainers, and in 1905 they were with Ted Holland's Vaudeville Company in Brisbane, but 1906 was their biggest year in their early career, the year they hit it big with a season at the Tivoli Theatre.

In March that year, the Carmos appeared at the Adelaide Tivoli supporting the sensational Le Roy, Talma and Bosco, a conjuring act that thrilled Australian audiences. Harry became firm friends with the trio and returned to Australia with them in 1914.

For the Tivoli, Harry and Nellie performed an array of juggling and balancing tricks which were warmly and enthusiastically embraced by audiences. In Melbourne, they were described as one of Harry Rickards's 'imported' acts, and for a brief time, they were the sensation of the Tivoli Circuit.

Harry dressed formally, and entered a stage set with a hat stand. He began by balancing the hat stand and throwing his gloves, hat and umbrella upon it, then Nellie was balanced on his head while she spun plates and Harry juggled balls. The most exciting part of the act was when Harry balanced Nellie on a stool which was held in his mouth. He then proceeded to walk up and down a flight of stairs with Nellie perched precariously above him. It was a 'novel and exceptionally clever juggling act' according to the newspaper.

The Carmos were so popular that Harry was interviewed in May by a Sydney paper. Harry told the paper that the feats of strength had cost him many strained muscles and a fractured arm. He mentioned that he had only been doing the act for three years, before which he was just a 'common' juggler.

> I saw that ordinary juggling turns were being overdone and I concluded that if I wished to get my head above the ruck I would have to do something out of the ordinary so I took on these balancing feats.

He added that his wife had complete confidence in him and that she needed to keep her head for the turn to be successful.

They completed 1906 with a season with Fullers in New Zealand, where their 'interesting combination of juggling and strength won them hearty applause'. After completing this engagement in 1907, they decided to sail for England for further work. Fullers was a step down from the Tivoli and there may have been better opportunities overseas.

Unfortunately, the ship they sailed on, the White Star Line *Suevic*, was wrecked off the coast of Cornwall. It was March, a foggy day, and the captain was speeding. The passengers had to abandon ship, women and children first, and all were successfully evacuated via lifeboat to land. The Carmos were fortunate and most of their props survived, although it must have been a harrowing experience.

They performed in England and France, but the relationship between Nellie and Harry was crumbling. He accused her of an affair in 1911, and in 1913 they divorced, and Harry married Rose Alice Pemberton, known as Alma May, a fellow performer. By this time, he was incorporating some magic into the show.

In 1914, Harry and Alma returned to Australia with Le Roy, Talma and Bosco. Billed as 'The Unknown' for reasons of 'policy', Harry opened the act. It was the same act he performed in 1906, with one change – in fact, many changes. The Unknown was billed as a protean juggler – a quick-change artist – so in between each feat, he would do a lightning-quick change of costume. He left the stage half a dozen times and returned in different clothes, and performed the ladder act, balanced Alma while she spun plates, and juggled three chairs.

The Unknown was, of course, known to many of the local artists, so Harry was identified by colleagues. However, the press kept mostly mum about his identity. The act was warmly received but overshadowed by the high-class skills of the main attraction, Le Roy, Talma and Bosco.

Harry soon left Australia again and travelled to the US with the conjurors. He was gaining experience as a magician and magic was his next adventure. After the First World War and into the 1920s, Harry became the Great Carmo, and his magic show toured the world.

After Alma's death in 1927, he started his own circus. He continued with it until the 1930s with varying degrees of success. During the Second World War, he and his assistant, Rita Rogers, soon to be the third Mrs Cameron, joined the entertainment corps with a magic show called 'Hey Presto'. Harry Cameron continued performing magic and juggling until his death in 1944 in England. He was apparently creating a juggling and magic show just before he died.

Conclusion

The death of Harry Rickards in 1911 meant that the Tivoli Circuit was sold to Hugh D. McIntosh, who concentrated on importing high-class vaudeville acts. When war broke out in 1914, McIntosh was in England scouting for talent, and found that many English artists were anxious to come to Australia for a much lower fee than usual. In 1914, both Cinquevalli and W.C. Fields made return visits. However, as the war dragged on, performers became scarce, not only due to conscription in England, but also due to travel problems. Women began to appear more frequently on stage as the men joined the war effort.

In 1917, the Australian government imposed an entertainment tax which made life even more difficult for theatre entrepreneurs. McIntosh of the Tivoli abandoned traditional variety/vaudeville for comedies, musicals and revues. By the time the war ended, the casualties were vast, and the plight of performers precarious, but jugglers kept juggling. However, times were changing. The moving pictures were becoming more popular and more cost-efficient, and live entertainment was slowly being replaced.

Many great jugglers visited Australia after the war, but the days of the headlining juggler were fast fading. The circus maintained the tradition and individual jugglers headlined long bills, but there was never another phenomenon like Cinquevalli.

Although the vaudeville theatres have disappeared, there are still jugglers performing today. They work at street fairs, in burlesque theatres, in traditional theatre and fringe festivals. Modern circuses usually include a juggler in their shows and the tradition of street juggling continues.

Juggling is a skill, an art and an exercise. Jugglers are passionate about their craft and generous with their skills, two characteristics that they've inherited from Cinquevalli, the Great Carmo, Lucy Gillet and all those that came before. Like them, they continue to innovate, create nd perform and will always do so while hands, feet and objects exist.

References

Before the British

Steve Cohen, 'The Juggling Girls of Tonga', *Whole Earth Review*, Spring 1988

Ken Edwards, 'Traditional games of a timeless land: play cultures in Aboriginal and Torres Strait Islander communities', *Australian Aboriginal Studies*, Vol. 2009, Issue 2, Fall 2009

Karl-Heinz Ziethen and Andrew Allen, *A Brief History of Juggling*, 1996, from Juggling Information Service, www.juggling.org viewed 29/1/21

Convict Jugglers

Peter Macfie, *Fiddlers & A Piper & Two Guitarists, Port Arthur as a Cultural Site & the Rare Inheritance of Musical Traditions in Tasmania*, Paper given at National Graduate Conference for Ethnomusicology, Faculty of Music, Cambridge University, July 2006, found at https://petermacfiehistorian.net.au/musicians/ viewed 28/1/20

Trish Symonds (compiler),

Joseph Crapp, https://www.opc-cornwall.org/Resc/emigrant_pdfs/crapp_joseph_1831.pdf, viewed 30/9/19

NSW Government Gazette, 24 April 1846, p. 512

The Early Circus Jugglers

Bell's *Life in Sydney and Sporting Reviewer*, Saturday 3 April 1852, p. 3

Nicola Brackertz, 'The battle for colonial circus supremacy: John Bull, Uncle Sam and their "Chariots of Fire"', *Australasian Drama Studies*, 35, October 1999

Bendigo Advertiser, Wednesday 27 May 1857, p. 3

Sydney Morning Herald, Friday 17 September 1852, p. 1

Bendigo Advertiser, Wednesday 27 May 1857, p. 3

Bell's *Life in Sydney and Sporting Reviewer*, Saturday 18 December 1852, p. 3

Riverine Herald, Saturday 1 January 1876, p. 3

Mark St Leon, *Circus: The Australian Story*, Melbourne

Books, Melbourne, Victoria, 2011, p. 29

Ibid., p 57.

Bathurst Free Press and Mining Journal, Wednesday 3 March 1852, p. 3

Mark St Leon, *Circus The Australian Story,* Melbourne Books, Melbourne, 2011, pp. 29–73

The Japanese Jugglers

D.C.S. Sissons, 'Immigration in Australian-Japanese Relations, 1871–1971', in J.A.A. Stockwin (ed.), *Japan and Australia in the Seventies*, Sydney, Angus and Robertson, 1972

Darryl Collins, 'Emperors and Musume, China and Japan "on the boards" in Australia, 1850s–1920s', in *East Asian History*, No. 7, June 1994, pp. 67–92

Tasmanian Times, Saturday 19 September 1868, p. 2

Argus, Wednesday 25 December 1867, p. 6

Tasmanian Times, Monday 18 May 1868, p. 2

Bendigo Advertiser, Saturday 29 February 1868, p. 2

Bendigo Advertiser, Monday 2 March 1868, p. 2

Adelaide Observer, Saturday 1 August 1868, p. 7

Tasmanian Times, Friday 22 May 1868, p. 2

Daily Telegraph, Wednesday 13 November 1901, p. 6

Bendigo Advertiser, Tuesday 25 February 1868, p. 2

South Australian Advertiser, Friday 14 August 1868, p. 2

Mount Alexander Mail, Saturday 5 September 1868, p. 2

Geelong Advertiser, Tuesday 14 March 1871, p. 3

Geelong Advertiser, Monday 16 December 1867, p. 3

Charles Waller, Gerald Taylor (eds), *Magical Nights at the Theatre,* Gerald Taylor Productions, 1980

'A Juggler not a Spy!', *Poverty Bay Herald*, Volume XXXVI, Issue 11826, 15 April 1909, p. 5

Raleigh Sun, Friday 9 April 1909, p. 2

The Minstrels

Richard Waterhouse, *From Minstrel Show to Vaudeville: The Australian Popular Stage 1788–1914,* New South Wales University Press, Sydney, 1990.

Bernard L. Peterson, Lena McPhatter Gore, *The African American Theatre Directory, 1816–1960: A Comprehensive Guide to Early Black Theatre Organizations, Companies, Theatres and Performing Groups*, Greenwood Press, 1997

Mercury, Monday 1 January
1900, p. 2

Advertiser, Wednesday 9 January
1901, p. 6

Evening News, Monday 26
November 1900, p. 8

Quiz, Thursday 7 February
1901, p. 14 (2)

Warragul Guardian, Friday 13
October 1899

Sydney Mail, Saturday 9 March
1901, p. 602 ????

Kalgoorlie Miner, Saturday 1
October 1898, p. 5

Daily News, Tuesday 30 August
1898, p. 3

Evening Journal, Monday 24
December 1900, p. 3

Sydney Morning Herald, Monday
16 April 1900, p. 7

*Gympie Times and Mary River
Mining Gazette*, Tuesday 30
January 1900, p. 3

Mercury, Monday 1 January
1900, p. 2

Advertiser, Tuesday 7 November
1899, p. 6

Express and Telegraph, Tuesday 7
November 1899, p. 4

Petersburg Times, Friday 10
November 1899, p. 4

Mercury, Saturday 30 December
1899, p. 3

The Ithaca Journal, Ithaca, NY,
USA, Thursday 28 February
1935

Cinquevalli

'Cinquevalli, the juggler. His
work and luck', *Referee*, 17
February 1909

Paul Cinquevalli,
http://www.juggling.org/fame/
cinquevalli/

Some Juggling Tales by Paul
Cinquevalli, *The Theatre*, 1
March 1909, p. 14

*Albury Banner and Wodonga
Express*, Friday 4 September
1914, p. 38

Bendigo Advertiser, Friday 18
April 1902, p. 4

Sporting Globe, Saturday 27
December 1941, p. 5

Ovens and Murray Advertiser,
Saturday 20 May 1899, p. 7

Argus, Thursday 28 September
1899, p. 6

Salerno

Table Talk, Thursday 6 March
1902, p. 14

Arena, Thursday 6 March 1902,
p. 11

David Cain, *Salerno: The
Inventive Gentleman Juggler,*
https:// juggle.org/salerno-the-
inventive-gentleman-juggler, 5
March 2015

Charles Waller, Gerald Taylor
(eds), *Magical Nights at the
Theatre,* Gerald Taylor
Productions, 1980

Kara

Daily Telegraph, Tuesday 4 April 1905, p. 3

Evening News, Tuesday 4 April 1905, p. 3

Sunday Sun, Sunday 21 May 1905, p. 1

Juggling Hall of Fame, Kara, http://www.juggling.org/fame/kara/index.html

Charles Waller, Gerald Taylor (eds), *Magical Nights at the Theatre,* Gerald Taylor Productions, 1980

W.C. Fields

Hebrew Standard of Australasia, Friday 31 July 1903, p. 11

Express and Telegraph, Monday 13 July 1903, p. 2

The Player, 15 September 1903

Rhodesia

Queenslander, Saturday 7 July 1900, p. 9

Otago Witness, NZ, 2 August 1905, p. 60

Free Lance, NZ, 13 June 1903, p. 14

Australian Town and Country Journal, Wednesday 16 October 1907, p. 40

Scone Advocate, Friday 17 August 1900, p. 2

The Lorgnette Observer, NZ 4 April 1901 p. 5

Brookhaven South Haven Hamlets and their people, http:// brookhavensouthhaven. org/hamletpeople/tng/getperson.php?personID=I12935&tree=hamlet

Kitty Harbeck

Sydney Morning Herald, Tuesday 28 October 1902, p. 6

West Australian, Monday 16 March, 1903, p. 3

Western Mail, Saturday 21 March 1903, p. 53

Death Notice, Mrs William A Harbeck, *New York Times*, 16 February 1936; ProQuest Historical Newspapers: *The New York Times,* p. N10

Punch, Thursday 18 December 1902, p. 32

Critic, Saturday 27 December 1902, p. 16

Newsletter: an Australian Paper for Australian People, Saturday 8 November 1902,

Cathrine Harbeck in household of William A. Harbeck, United States Census, 1910, FamilySearch.org

William A. Harbeck, United States Census, 1910, FamilySearch. org

Catherine Harbeck, New York Passenger Lists, 1820–1891, FamilySearch.org

William Harbeck in household of Pheebe Harbeck, United States Census, 1880, FamilySearch. org

Charles Waller, Gerald Taylor (eds), *Magical Nights at the Theatre,* Gerald Taylor Productions, 1980

Lucy Gillett

'A Lady Cinquevalli. Clever Lucy Gillet Astounds Tivoli Patrons,' *The Mail*, 16 August 1913, p. 5

'A Marvellous Juggler', *Sydney Mail and NSW Advertiser,* 1 July 1899, p. 23

'In Fashions Realm, What to Wear Up to Date Notes', *Western Mail,* 3 January 1913, p. 4

'Noted Lady Juggler', *The World's News*, 14 June 1913, p. 5

'Paul Cinquevalli Away from the Footlights', *Table Talk*, 13 August 1914

Peter Quines, 'Theatre Royal', *Punch*, 17 July 1913, p. 37

Quiz, 9 January 1913, p. 3

'Sydney Shows', *Punch*, 19 June, 1913, p. 15

David Cain, Updates of David Cain's Past Articles 2014, https://www.juggle.org/updates-of-david-cains-past-articles

Frank Van Straten, *Tivoli*, Thomas Lothian, Melbourne, 2003

Charles Waller, Gerald Taylor (eds), *Magical Nights at the Theatre,* Gerald Taylor Productions, 1980

Selma Braatz

Unassisted passenger lists Victoria (1852–1923), Record Series Number (VPRS):947, https://prov.vic.gov.au/explore-collection/explore-topic/passenger-records-and-immigration/unassisted-passenger-lists

The Adelaide Register, 4 March 1914

The Argus, 5 January 1914.

Charles Waller, Gerald Taylor (eds), *Magical Nights at the Theatre,* Gerald Taylor Productions, 1980

The Referee newspaper, 11 February 1914

Club Juggling in Australia

Tom Breen 'Juggling Firsts' *Jugglers Bulletin*, No. 20 Juggling Information Service 1946, http://www.juggling.org/jb/jb20.html

David Cain, *Juggling Props: A History*, Vol. 1, David Cain, USA, 2017

Marizles Wirth, Diary

Derenda and Breen

Express and Telegraph, Tuesday 7 November 1899, p. 4

Evening Journal, Monday 14 April 1902, p. 4

Newsletter: an Australian Paper for Australian People, Saturday 11 January 1902

Sportsman, Wednesday 26 March 1902, p. 3

Evening Journal, Monday 14 April, 1902, p. 4

Charles Waller, Gerald Taylor (eds), *Magical Nights at the Theatre*, Gerald Taylor Productions, 1980

West Australian, Wednesday 16 September 1908, p. 9

Selbo

Age, Monday 19 November 1906, p. 5

Evening Star, Wednesday 17 April 1907, p. 4

Daily Telegraph, Monday 31 December 1906, p. 7

Victoria and Albert Museum, http://collections.vam.ac.uk/item/O1152171/hanging-card-unknown/

Charles Waller, Gerald Taylor (eds), *Magical Nights at the Theatre*, Gerald Taylor Productions, 1980

The Geraldos

Evening Star, Tuesday 26 November 1907, p. 4

Australian Star, Monday 19 August 1907, p. 8,

Sun, Sunday 4 April 1909, p. 12

Charles Waller, Gerald Taylor (eds), *Magical Nights at the Theatre*, Gerald Taylor Productions, 1980

Morris Cronin

Punch, Thursday 18 August 1910, p. 38

Daily Herald, Monday 1 August 1910, p. 2

Daily Herald, Wednesday 19 October 1910, p. 7

Sydney Sportsman, Wednesday 21 September 1910, p. 2

Prahran Telegraph, Saturday 24 September 1910, p. 2

Sunday Sun, Sunday 25 September 1910, p. 13

Age, Monday 15 August 1910, p. 8

Table Talk, Thursday 25 August 1910, p. 21

Sun, Monday 19 September 1910, p. 3

US Passport Applications, Morris Cronin, 1906–1907, roll 0031 certificates 2701-28400 from ancestry.com

Marizles Wirth

Marizles Wirth Martin, Diary, ca 1885–1903 State Library of NSW, Sydney, Australia

Rachel Fensham, 'Making-real the body: a subordinate reading of the female performer', *Australasian Drama Studies*, 1 April 1997: 30

Evening News, Thursday 12 May 1881, p. 3

Wagga Wagga Advertiser, Saturday 4 September 1909, p. 5

Queenslander, Saturday 2 October 1915, p. 29

Ballarat Star, Tuesday 30 August 1887, p. 4

Telegraph, Wednesday 10 June 1891, p. 5

Daily News, Monday 13 August 1900, p. 2

Leader, Friday 27 February 1914, p. 1

Philip Wirth, *The life of Philip Wirth: a lifetime with an Australian circus, 1935*, https://nla.gov.au:443/tarkine/nla.obj-44149096

Mark St Leon, email correspondence, 2021

The Lentons

Truth, Saturday 11 February 1905, p. 7

Referee, Wednesday 12 March 1902, p. 10

Daily Telegraph, Monday 6 January 1896, p. 6

Sydney Morning Herald, Monday 10 March 1902, p. 3

Daily Telegraph, Saturday 14 December 1895, p. 9

Australian Star, Monday 10 March 1902, p. 3

Daily Telegraph, Monday 10 March 1902, p. 3

Sunday Times, Sunday 9 March 1902, p. 2

Newsletter: an Australian Paper for Australian People, Saturday 15 March 1902

Otago Daily Times, NZ, Issue 12256, 21 January 1902

Evening Star, NZ, Issue 11661, 21 January 1902

Myra Kemble, Benefit Programme, 1896

Mishaps and misdeeds

Age, Tuesday 14 January 1902, p. 7

Sydney Mail and New South Wales Advertiser, Wednesday 25 May 1904, p. 1289????

Evening News, Wednesday 18 May 1904, p. 5

Evening News, Friday 23 September 1904, p. 7

Truth, Sunday 21 February 1904, p. 6

Evening News, Monday 7 November 1904, p. 3

New South Wales Police Gazette and Weekly Record of Crime, Wednesday 25 May, 1904

Darling Downs Gazette, Tuesday 10 May 1904, p. 3

Singleton Argus, Saturday 4 June 1904, p. 3

The Australian Vaudeville Jugglers

Arnold Jarvis

Register, Monday 19 August 1901, p. 3

Western Mail, Saturday 2 February 1901, p. 51

Express and Telegraph, Saturday 30 September 1899, p. 5

Truth, Saturday 19 August 1911, p. 10

North-Eastern Advertiser, Friday 10 June 1910, p. 2

Evening Journal, Wednesday 21 August 1901, p. 3

Robert G. Molyneux, *The Arnold Jarvis Story,* Highton, Victoria, R.G. Molyneux, 1986

Anglo the Juggler

Chronicle, Saturday 5 March 1904, p. 33

Register, Monday 29 February 1904, p. 5

Evening Journal, Monday 29 February 1904, p. 2

Advertiser, Saturday 31 May 1902, p. 10

Albury Banner and Wodonga Express, Friday 4 March 1904, p. 34

Register, Wednesday 28 May 1902, p. 8

Evening Journal, Friday 30 May 1902, p. 4

Express and Telegraph, Tuesday 1 March 1904, p. 4

Sunday Times, Sunday 6 March 1904, p. 8

Quiz, Friday 6 June 1902, p. 7

Advertiser, Tuesday 1 March 1904, p. 7

Evening Journal, Thursday 14 April 1904, p. 1

Advertiser, Friday 13 May 1904, p. 6

Express and Telegraph, Thursday 12 May 1904, p. 1

Express and Telegraph, Thursday 14 April 1904, p. 1

Niels Duinker (ed.), *Thomas 'Anglo' Horton – The art of modern Juggling,* 2019

Lennon Hyman Lennon

Brisbane Courier, Tuesday 28 November 1905, p. 6

Daily Telegraph, Monday 18 March 1901, p. 3

Lyttlton Times, NZ, Volume CV, Issue 12423, 12 February 1901, p. 2

Brisbane Courier, Tuesday 28 November 1905, p. 6

Mercury, Monday 3 October 1904, p. 5

Barrier Miner, Friday 8 October 1909, p. 8

Daily Telegraph, 18 May 1895, p. 6

Sport, Friday 11 December 1925, p. 8

Sinbad the Sailor, broadsheet/advertising 1906

Sinbad the Sailor, pantomime program 1906

The Kavanaghs

Referee, Wednesday 12 May 1915, p. 15

Referee, Wednesday 18 January 1911, p. 15

Barrier Miner, Monday 27 July 1914, p. 8

Examiner, Wednesday 5 September 1923, p. 5

Referee, Wednesday 9 February 1916, p. 15

Referee, Wednesday 23 August 1916, p. 14

Referee, Wednesday 17 September 1913, p. 16

Sunday Times, Sunday 3 February 1918, p. 15

Victorian Marriage Certificate, Arthur Kavanagh, 1887, No 2920

Victorian Birth Certificate, Arthur Stanilaus Kavanagh, 1889, No 27088

Victorian Birth Certificate, Francis Kavanagh, 1887, No 25215

Petition for US Naturalisation, Stan Kavanagh, no 375548 1924, via ancestry.com

Freeman's Journal, Thursday 13 July 1911, p. 29

Barrier Miner, Friday 1 May 1908, p. 4

Sun, Saturday 12 May 1951, p. 5

Mirror, Saturday 12 January 1924, p. 8

Table Talk, Thursday 30 April 1936, p. 16

Grenfell Record and Lachlan District Advertiser, Monday 22 October 1923, p. 2

Daily Herald, Monday 13 August 1923, p. 2

Examiner, Saturday 15 September 1923, p. 14

Maud Florence and Victor Martyn

Telegraph, Thursday 13 June 1895, p. 5

Telegraph, Friday 7 December 1894, p. 5

Telegraph, Friday 29 January 1897, p. 5

Telegraph, Monday 8 February 1897, p. 5

Queenslander, Saturday 31 March 1894, p. 582 ???

Truth, Sunday 30 December 1894, p. 2

Queensland Times, Ipswich Herald and General Advertiser, Thursday 9 October 1902, p. ????

Punch, Thursday 2 May 1901, p. 27

Brisbane Courier, Friday 14 June 1895, p. 4

Telegraph, Monday 11 December 1899, p. 4

Daily Mercury, Monday 14 November 1910, p. 6

Daily Mercury, Thursday 10 November 1910, p. 4

Sydney Morning Herald, Wednesday 20 November 1907, p. 12

Evening Telegraph, Tuesday 21 May 1912, p. 3

Sunday Times, Sunday 24 March 1912, p. 2

Evening Journal, Saturday 9 April 1910, p. 7

Register, Saturday 25 May 1907, p. 6

Daily Telegraph, Monday 10 August 1908, p. 4

Daily Herald, Monday 25 April 1910, p. 6

Daily Mercury, Saturday 12 November 1910, p. 4

Evening Telegraph, Monday 20 May 1912, p. 3

Sunday Mail, Sunday 22 September 1929, p. 12

Labor Daily, Wednesday 4 September 1929, p. 7

Herald, Tuesday 10 September 1929, p. 17

Sun, Sunday, 14 June 1908, p. 7

Newsletter: an Australian Paper for Australian People, Saturday 29 February 1908

Northam Advertiser, Wednesday 6 May 1908, p. 2

Kalgoorlie Miner, Tuesday 9 June 1908, p. 6

Truth, Saturday 2 May 1908, p. 8

Morning Bulletin, Wednesday 23 November 1910, p. 2

Newsletter: an Australian Paper for Australian People, Saturday 20 August 1910

Sydney Sportsman, Wednesday 15 September 1909, p. 3

Herald, Monday 6 September 1909, p. 4

Northern Miner, Monday 20 May 1912, p. 4

Sun, Friday 1 December 1911, p. 6

Daily Telegraph, Saturday 3 June 1911, p. 12

Herald, Tuesday 10 September 1929, p. 17

Daily Mercury, Monday 14 November 1910, p. 6

Victorian Marriages, Victor Martin, Mary Maud Thyers

NSW Births, Decima Martyn

Queensland birth records, Mary Maud Thyers

Letter William Zavis to Topper Martyn 22 January 1978 from www.conjuringarts.org

The Great Carmo

Ballarat Star, Monday 9 July 1906, p. 1

Sunday Sun, Sunday 20 May 1906, p. 5

Newcastle Morning Herald and Miners' Advocate, Saturday 31 March 1906, p. 14

Ballarat Star, Monday 9 July 1906, p. 1

Sunday Sun, Sunday 20 May 1906, p. 5

Newcastle Morning Herald and Miners' Advocate, Saturday 31 March 1906, p. 14

Argus, Monday 26 March 1906, p. 8

Brisbane Courier, Friday 14 April 1905, p. 4

Brisbane Courier, Thursday 20 April 1905, p. 2

Brisbane Courier, Friday 28 August 1903, p. 5

Brisbane Courier, Monday 31 August 1903, p. 5

Geelong Advertiser, Thursday 10 October 1901, p. 3

Sydney Morning Herald, Saturday 23 November 1901, p. 2

Evening Echo, Monday 29 June 1914, p. 4

Argus, Monday 6 July 1914, p. 13

Geelong Advertiser, Friday 11 October 1901, p. 4

Newsletter: an Australian Paper for Australian People, Saturday 9 August 1902

Gadfly, Wednesday 7 March 1906, p. 10

Gadfly, Wednesday 28 March 1906, p. 10

Sunday Times, Sunday 24 July 1904, p. 2

Sydney Sportsman, Wednesday 7 May 1902, p. 8

Tasmanian News, Saturday 24 December 1904, p. 2

Kalgoorlie Miner, Monday 5 February 1906, p. 4

Referee, Wednesday 23 January 1907, p. 12

Truth, Sunday 10 February 1907, p. 4

Scrutineer and Berrima District Press, Wednesday 20 March 1907, p. 2

Herald, Monday 6 July, 1914, p. 8 ate (NSW: 1876–1954), Friday 31 May 1907, p. 4

Star, Christchurch, NZ, Issue 8742, 2 October 1906, p. 1

Evening Post, NZ, Vol LXXIII, issue 109, 9 May 190, p. 6

The Great Carmo, Juggler, Magician, circus owner, Programs and related material collected by the National Library of Australia

Val Andrews, *The Great Carmo, The Colossus of Mystery*, 2001

Charles Waller, Gerald Taylor (eds), *Magical Nights at the Theatre,* Gerald Taylor Productions, 1980

Conclusion

Frank Van Straten, *Tivoli*, Thomas Lothian, Melbourne, 2003

Picture Credits

Page 49: Marizles Wirth, courtesy of Mark St Leon
Page 59: Arnold (Arnoldi) Jarvis, courtesy of Brenton Maile

CPSIA information can be obtained
at www.ICGtesting.com
Printed in the USA
LVHW032043100522
718323LV00014B/469